11/19/00 MA
GOD
TO BL

HMOS 3.3

RODNEY K. DIGGS

"HOW THE PRECIOUS SONS OF ZION, ONCE WORTH THEIR WEIGHT IN GOLD, ARE NOW CONSIDERED AS POTS OF CLAY, THE WORK OF A POTTER'S HANDS!" - LAMENTATIONS 4:2 (NIV)

ZION'S MEN

Compiled and Edited By Rodney K. Diggs

ZION'S MEN
ISBN 9- 70382-308

Published by
JWWALKER MINISTRIES, INC
9 Music Square South, Suite 321
Nashville, Tennessee 37205

ZION'S MEN

Compiled and Edited by
Rodney K. Diggs

JWWalker Ministries, Inc.
Nashville, Tennessee

ACKNOWLEDGEMENTS

I want to thank my lovely and God-centered wife, Zenola for her unwavering support during this project.

Thank you to my two biggest "Heroes", Levester Boykin and Kenneth H. Diggs for your lifetime support , wisdom and guidance. To my Mom, the "Sparkplug" of the Diggs clan, thanks for the courage to "press-on".

I wish to thank my Pastor, Bishop Joseph Warren Walker, III for being that beacon on the shore of progress and the greatest Pastor this side of heaven. I love you, Man!

Thanks to the male Elders and Ministers of Mt. Zion Baptist Church, who's sermons and poems make up the body of this project. Thanks to "Zion's Men", my co-laborers in Christ.

A special thanks to Kenneth and Minister Elisa Baptiste for proofreading this manuscript.

CONTENTS

MINISTER ALEX D. ATKINSON

"CAIN AND ABEL"

(GENESIS 4:1-18)

Here we have Cain and Abel the first sons of Adam and Eve. Cain and Abel, brother vs. brother our first showing of sibling rivalry in the Bible. If we look at the story of Cain and Abel, brother vs. brother, our first killing in the Bible. How did we get to the point that we have brother killing brother? How did we get off track that people would kill without thinking of the consequences? Brother vs. Brother, church member vs. church member, and even parent vs. child is where we are today. The biblical story of Cain and Abel is famous in the archives of preaching and you can't go to heaven without hearing stories such as these (like....Job and the 3 Hebrew boys). As we examine this story and if I had to put a tag on this text, today we are going to talk about The Gift or the Giver.

This story begins with Adam and Eve the happy couple of the Garden of Eden and their sons Cain and Abel. The first kids of the Garden of Eden. There comes a time for Cain and Abel to make an offering to the Lord. We see Cain and Abel at the altar of God making their sacrificial offering to the Lord. It is in the text .....in verse (3), "And in the process of time it came to pass, that Cain brought of the fruit of the ground an offering unto the Lord." Cain gives his offering and Abel gives his offering. Abel gives from the fatted portions, while Cain gives from the normal portions. God says good job to Abel's gift and rejects Cain's offering.

So too many of us are in the question : Gift or the Giver?

To many, Cain had given what seems to be his best, but the

text shows us that he could have done better, because the Lord in verse (7) states "if you do well, will you not be accepted?". That if you put your best foot forward will not God honor that and receive your offering. This is not just a question on what God is looking for in our offering? God does not play favorites he is not a respecter of person. He is not only looking for what was given, but also in the attitude that it was given. God can look past just the gift to the heart of the giver. For the scriptures claim where a person's heart is, his treasure lies also.

Two boys were trying out for the champion football team and the coach only has one more slot. One is an excellent ball handler; the other one is excellent on defense and a team player. The coach chooses the team player over the ball handler, because he sees past the athletic ability to what will benefit the team when it comes down to the wire. Cain upset over being rejected by God for no apparent reason, lets emotions take control and invites Abel to the field. We as Christians must remember that Sin is always Lurking. This was an invitation to death and non-existence, to some degree our first premeditated murder in the world. Sin has managed to take control of the actions of Cain and resulted in the murder of Abel.

We must always be careful that emotions do not over take us. So many Christians are quick to always let emotions run their lives. As soon as someone cuts us off on the freeway, we utter out hateful words then ,"thank you Jesus", for not having the accident. Sin some days comes from those dark places, lurking in the shadows. Sin is always looking for Christians, who have let down their guard. Satan our adversary is always looking for ways to divide the body of Christ. Sin some days is like a lion hunting for prey , Christians. Too many of our brothers

and sisters (i.e. Cain) have been easy pickings for sin. We must always be on the defensive watch.
The Church needs to be on alert because the devil is out for the kill.

Cain has committed evil before the Lord. God has questioned not only Cain's credibility, but also his love for his own brother. God plays detective and investigates the murder of Abel, and soon becomes judge to deliver justice on Cain for this unmerciful act. Cain begins to beg the Lord for his life because of his wrong doings. That is just like so many Christians today, once we have done wrong and the Lord catches us in it. We then try to beg for forgiveness and protection from the Lord. Cain in verse 13 ....is begging for his life and for God's protection and provision. Isn't it interesting that when we are doing the wrong we are not looking for God, but when the wrong catches up with us God is needed? Even in the Curse there is a Blessing. God decides not only to punish Cain, but like a parent, to continue to provide protection and provision for him.

Many would question, "how do you get the blessing from the same God that cursed you". A loving parent, in disciplining their children always reminds them it is out of love. The fact that God is like a loving parent gives us some comfort and joy. You can always envision God's Loving arms around you, even when God has to punish you. The blessing lies in the fact that the love is shown. The church can learn a lesson from the forgiveness of Cain by God. If we are to love our neighbors as ourselves, then forgiveness is an important key. The path where the world has gone wrong so many times, is the place the church must be willing to correct in loving one another even when we see wrong has been done.

The blessing comes in learning how to turn the other cheek, to pray for those that would do evil against us, and even showing love to those that misuse us. This is what we can learn from the story of Cain and Abel. That the church should not be playing favorites in dealing with people and lives, because the enemy is always out there in dark places, ready to attack us (i.e. you and me) like prey. We must remember to watch for one another and show some love when one of our brothers and sisters stumbles along this Christian journey.

Minister Alex D. Atkinson was born in Chattanooga, Tennessee on May 11, 1974 to Charles Duke and Ingria A. Grier. Alex was educated at Chattanooga's Brainerd High School in 1992, graduated with a Bachelor of Electrical Engineering degree, 1996 from Vanderbilt University, has earned a Masters of Business Administration in Marketing and Finance from Tennessee State University. Alex will receive a second master's degree, a Masters of Divinity from Vanderbilt University in 2001.

Minister Atkinson was baptized at Wesley Chapel Community Church of Chattanooga, Tennessee, where Pastor Herbert H. Wright serves as Senior Pastor. Bishop Joseph W. Walker, III, licensed Alex at Mt. Zion Baptist Church-Nashville in 1998. He has served in various area of Ministry, including overseer of the 1,500 member College Ministry at Mt. Zion Baptist Church. Alex currently serves as Adjutant to Bishop Walker at the Mt. Zion Church. He is a member of several organizations including Kappa Alpha Psi Fraternity, Inc.

Elder K. Edwin Bryant

"Help Me Somebody"

(Acts 20: 7-10)

"And upon the first day of the week, when the disciples came together to break bread, Paul preached unto them, ready to depart on the morrow; and continued his speech until midnight. And there were many lights in the upper chamber, where they were gathered together. And there sat in a window a certain young man named Eutychus, being fallen into a deep sleep: and as Paul was long preaching, he sunk down with sleep, and fell down from the third loft, and was taken up dead. And Paul went down, and fell on him, and embracing him said trouble not yourselves; for his life is in him. (KJV)

I realize that we all have been in situations where we needed help and I believe Eutychus' cry for help is based upon his:

I. Placement

He is sitting in a dangerous place - he was comfortable settling for a seat in a dangerous position. He bypassed all other possible options. Instead of trying to squeeze on the end of the pew, instead of trying to find a place along the wall to stand, the first place he chose was the window. I want to raise a question. Why are we attracted to dangerous things? Why are we attracted to someone else's spouse when we know good and well that they'll never leave them for us - That's dangerous! What causes us to be attracted to people who abuse us? How is it that we can think of so many ways to steal what we want, instead of just trusting God at his word? I don't know, but I do know this- Any counselor would agree with me when I say people who prefer something dangerous, over something safe, are crying out for help.

He was sitting under the Word - (Paul was preaching). I hear Eutychus crying for help because he is sitting under the Word, sitting under an awesome anointing, but he still remains in a dangerous place. I can identify with Eutychus - even though I sit under the Word every week, I still find myself passing up something that's good for me in order to get something that's bad. And I think this is a prime example of being in the right place, but the wrong location. Despite the bad decision he made by sitting in the window, I must give him credit for at least coming to worship. However, since I am required to preach the truth, just coming to worship is not enough. A lot of us get caught up in coming to church. Now who is the church? We are! So in other words, a lot of us get hung up on coming to see each other. A lot of us are in the right place, but in the wrong location. Instead of coming to worship and positioning yourself around people moving towards holiness, some of us tend to migrate towards hell raisers. Marriage is the right place for a lot of us, but we picked up our spouse in the wrong location. God intended for many of us to be homeowners, but some of us walk the floors all night trying to figure out how we are going to pay the mortgage, you're in the right house but the wrong location. We all have been guilty of being in the right place, but the wrong location. Not only is his cry for help based on placement, but his cry for help also comes from his:

II. Predicament

He fell asleep because the Word became repetitious - sometimes when we come to church and hear sermons that have a common theme, we tend not to listen closely because we feel as if we have heard the sermon before. It's one thing to think you know the Word, but it is another to discover that you don't. The preacher can be preaching, but because we think we are stronger than we really are, we stop paying attention. When we stop paying attention to the preached Word, our minds start to wander. When we wander outside of God's will, we are subject to drift into areas where we shouldn't be. When our minds start to wander, we slowly expose who we really are. And in order to stay undetected, we become sneaky. Some of us think that we are getting away with it on the "DL", or "QT" or any other name you want to use to disguise your sin; unfortunately, we're not. In verse 8, the text says that they were on the third floor, it was dark, and there were a lot of lights in the room and Eutychus was sitting in the window. Sin is a dark place, and Christians are the light of the world. Even though the devil has deceived you into thinking that you are in the dark, you're not. Sin doesn't destroy our light, it dims it. So even the faintest light can expose your life. This is the same reason why a lot of us have lost our ability to witness, too many people saw us do too many things that we shouldn't have. You better be careful because the Bible declares that what you do in secret, will one day be yelled from the roof top.

He also fell asleep because the conditions in the room were favorable for sleeping - In this text, lights equal lamps. A lamp uses oil to burn. The fumes from the lamps had the potential to cause drowsiness. And the heat from the lamps made conditions favorable for sleeping. Eutychus could have fallen asleep because of the fumes and the heat in the room. But, I want to suggest that Eutychus should have never fallen asleep. Eutychus' sitting in the window to me was a cry for help. He chose to sit somewhere that was unsafe. I want to argue today that the people Eutychus went to worship with, helped cause his predicament. Eutychus had a whole lot of company, but no spiritual companions.

How can we not help someone that is about to make a terrible mistake? Why don't we minister to people when you see that they are headed for destruction? What causes us not to be concerned with how your Christian brothers and sisters chose to live their lives? Do you think that its easier to let them make the decision for themselves? Sometimes it is. But, there are other times when we can jump in but we don't. We just sit back and say we'll let them deal with their hang-ups in their own time. Allowing someone to deal with it in their own time may not be enough time. But the real issue is that sometimes in the privacy of our own homes, we become grateful that we are not in the situation that our so called friends are in. But baby, you better learn a few lessons from Noah and his son. Noah was drunk one day and one of his sons came in and found him exposed, but when the other son found out about the condition his daddy was in, he got a sheet, he walked backwards into the room and covered his father. You better think twice about not covering someone in his or her time of need because the time might come when someone might need to throw a sheet over you.

His fall exposed his problem - Eutychus fell not because of where he was, but because of what he was doing when he fell. If he had fallen asleep any where else, he probably would have never been mentioned. He experienced a public fall, whereas many of us when we do fall, we fall in private. Private falls allow you to conceal, but public falls force you to reveal. Oh, it's a dangerous thing when your private life becomes public. I wish I had time to develop this, but I must move on. The last thing I want to lift up in this text is his Plight - his distressing situation.

III. Plight

Even though this young man's situation looks distressing, the spiritual people around Eutychus rose to the occasion. And in responding to Eutychus, he gave you and I a formula that we can use to help restore anyone that has fallen. He went down, he was personal (he stopped what he was doing). He fell on him- he was passionate (they ministered to them without prejudice). He didn't criticize the boy, he just helped him up. He didn't need to know what he did wrong, the fall had already done that. He just needed someone to be a friend, someone to believe in him again. He embraced him, he was persistent. His helping him was not contingent upon whether he was wrong or right. But it was based upon the fact that he had fallen and he needed someone to help him up. Has anyone ever fallen before? Has anyone ever told you that you could never be what God intended you to be? Have you ever been told that something you were working on could not be done? I remember some years ago, I was sitting in a window, I was sitting in a dangerous place. I was married to someone that I should have never been with and I began to fall into a deep spiritual sleep. I was helping to raise a child, only to find out later that the little girl was not mine. Oh lord, oh lord, that incident alone caused me to fall. As I fell, within my marriage, I experienced every type of abuse there is. I was hurting, I was damaged and distraught! I did not know if I was coming or if I was going. When I filed for divorce, I hit the ground. I felt like my life had been ruined; and I was told that I would never be what I once was. But, someone made the mistake by saying to me, that whatever I tried from that point on couldn't be done. "Somebody said it couldn't be done". Oh, I made it; Oh I made it, Oh...I made it.

K. Edwin (Kerry) Bryant is a native of Elyria, Ohio and a recent graduate of American Baptist College in Nashville, Tennessee. Kerry currently serves as the Chief Operating Officer at Mt. Zion Baptist Church-Nashville and as a solid role model for all the Associate Ministers. He and his wife, Sonja are expecting their first child in early 2001.

Minister Brandon L. Davis

"Aren't Tired of Folk?"

(2 Corinthians 4:8)

You know Christian folk; acting like everything is all right all the time. Every time you see some folk, they are just phony as a nickel with a black president on it. Just phony.., never really testifying, just test-a-lying... You know piggy backing on someone else's experience.

When many times the truth of the matter is, we smile to cover up the truth, but we should "let our light so shine, though our affliction to let men see our good works and glorify our father which is in heaven". 2 Corinthians 4:8 NIV

The truth is, we are troubled on every side. yet not distressed: we are perplexed but not in despair; persecuted, but not forsaken; cast down, but not destroyed; Always bearing about in the body the dying of the Lord Jesus, that the life also of Jesus might be made manifest in our body.

We need to just be real. Don't be afraid to admit it's hard right through here.
Temptations and trials, come in multitudes sometimes. And sometimes I'm gonna look at you and say Pray for Me.

The thing I love so much about God is that for every sin, temptation or situation He provides a way of escape.
And ultimately He offers help and hope in Him.

In 2 Corinthians 4:17 it states...
Dark times, we are afflicted
For our light affliction, which is but for a moment, its just

for a moment.. This too shall pass.
How long is our affliction?
Who does it work for, us?
What are the benefits?
For us, all things work for us.
A far more exceeding and eternal weight of glory;

Meaning this little trial you are going through now, that you've been losing sleep over, God says "go to sleep. I never sleep nor slumber". It does not compare to the glory that awaits them that endure, them that love Him.

Our big problem though is Verse 18... if we could just remember this when that man he says he leaving you, or when the job gave you the pink slip... it doesn't matter what it looks like.., quit trippin, stop focusing on carnal things, we are in a war and you are trippin over what you see.

"Come for Me !!"

Maybe I am being hasty. I may be a little crazy.

I know you do things in your time.
But Lord this world is very unkind.

How long do I have to sit. I am very tired I admit.

Though you say I should faint not. Often I'm filled with doubt.

Lord how do you see me.
Am I one of your beautiful trees.

I hold my arms up in worship to you.

But my arms are weak, am I getting through.

I have done your work.
Or is there something else.
Am I to blame for my sad times.
Or is this a test, to strengthen my mind.

I like it here, my families great, my church is
Fine but it's getting late.
I've been here long enough now, I've done my work
I need a ride, to leave this earth

Oh Come for me.
Take me up in the clouds.
Can we meet like you promised?
Is my mansion ready?
Oh come for me.

Blessed Lord Jesus.
Rapture me.
I'm tired
Can I see you soon?
Will I leave from my room?
Will I be in Church?
Will I be on the street? Will I be in my car?
Where ever, when ever, Please "Come for Me!!"
come for me. Blessed Lord Jesus.
By Brandon L. Davis

Minister Brandon L. Davis

BL was born in Cleveland, Ohio, the son of Anderson and Frances Davis. His home church is Temple Baptist Church of Cleveland Ohio. BL attended the Pilgrim Emannuel Baptist Church in Nashville, Tennessee, where he received his call to ministry under Pastor Roderick C. Pounds.

Minister Davis accepted his call to ministry in August, 1996 and preached his first sermon on January 26, 1997. BL has been a member of the Mt. Zion Baptist Church for 2 years and currently serves as the Overseer for the Outreach Ministry. BL's interests are basketball, song writing, singing and last but not least studying the Word of God.

Minister Tommie E. Davis

"Preacher, What's Your Burden?"

1. Introduction

A. The great Dr. M. L. Scott, Jr. is reported to have said, "The preacher who does not have a Burden is a preacher who cannot legitimately preach."

B. In other words, effective, authentic and prophetic preaching only comes from those preachers who may have not only been licensed, ordained, educated and "credentialized", but it comes from those preachers who have been "Burdenized"!!

C. That is to say that preachers who have made a difference have always had a "Burden"! Such preachers as John Bunyan, Martin Luther King, Jr., John Wesley, Wilberforce, Roger Williams, Richard Allen, Charles H. Spurgeon were all men with a "Burden".

2. Definition of the Preacher's Burden

A. The Preacher's Burden may be understood as special, deep and compelling concern and/or assignment that possesses him, disturbs him, drives him to expression and action in spite of his frail humanity.

B. Many times the preacher's call and commission itself is a "Burden".

1. *Look at Isaiah 6: 1-8*

2. *Look at Jeremiah 1:4-10*

3. *Look at Jonah 1: 1-3 and 3:1-2*

4. *Look at Hosea 1:2-11 & 14*

5. *Look at 1 Corinthian 9:16*

3. Outstanding Personalities Who Can Be Characterized By Their "Burdens"

A. Most religious and moral philosophical figures of gigantic stature were and are persons who have operated under the weight of a pressing "burden".

1. Socrates had a burden for Truth and Virtue.
2. Dietrich Bonhoeffer had a burden for making Christianity relevant to one's contemporary situation.
3. Mother Teresa had a burden for the destitute and dying in India and the world over.
4. Bishop Desmond Tutu has a burden for freeing black South Africans.
5. Dr. Martin Luther King, Jr. had a burden for obtaining the full Civil Right for Black and poor people in the United States.
6. Rev. Jessie Jackson has a burden for morally sensitizing this nation.

B. A Closer Look at Jesus and His Burden(s)

1. Make no mistake about it. Jesus Christ himself was driven and possessed by certain pronounced "Burdens"!
2. Scriptural Examples
    a. Look at Luke 4:16-18

b. Look at Luke 19:10
c. Look at Mark 10:45
d. Look at Matthew 26:39

4. The Contemporary Tragedy of "Burdenless Preachers.

A. I submit to you that the Black Church today is in a crisis precisely because too many Black pulpits are occupied by Preachers who have no real "burdens".

B. For far too many Preachers are caught up in cars, clothes, costume jewelry, pride, popularity, positions, bucks, broads and buildings, instead of being redemptively arrested by some "burden" from the Lord!

C. What Does A "Burdenless" Preacher Look Like?
1. Burdenless Preachers are Preachers who have little or no sense of accountability to the God who called them.
2. Burdenless Preachers are Preachers who preach to please; they preach to entertain; they preach to indulge the people in maintaining a superficial religion.
3. Burdenless Preachers are Preachers who use people, take advantage of people, lie to people and steal from people.
4. Burdenless Preachers are Preachers who believe in taking short cuts, who believe in cutting corners, who believe in sliding and trying to get by with as little effort as possible!
5. Burdenlesss Preachers are Preachers who are so into money; who are so into drinking liquor; who are so into snorting dope; who are so into being "ecclesiastical Don Juans", until they have become comatose to the demands of a vibrant and authentic Ministry!
6. Burdenless Preachers are Preachers who are lazy Preachers, greedy Preachers, selfish Preachers; they are

Preachers who are self-satisfied!

5. The Existential "Burdens" of The Preacher

A. The Preacher's very existence and task is constituted by several built-in burdens.

B. For the called Preacher not only has the awesome burden of his assignment to preach the Gospel in spirit and in truth, but the

C. Preacher also has the burden of his flesh; the burden of his fears and the burden of his faith.

1. The Preacher's Burden of His Flesh
a. As if the task of preaching the Gospel were not enough, the Preacher must constantly deal with the insurrection of their flesh.

b. For the flesh (fleshly desires, fleshly thoughts, fleshly involvements, etc.) consistently declares war on the Preachers' concentration as they attempt to express his burden.

c. Look at Paul the Preacher and the burden of his flesh (Romans 7:19-24).

2. The Preachers' Burden of His Fears
a. All conscientious Preachers are forever being hounded by the fears of insecurity, rejection, incompetence, and not being able to live up to the task of credible preaching the Gospel.

b. For fear of fears are the constant companions of Preachers who have a burden. See Isaiah 6:5, 1Kings 19: 1-

5, Ephesians 3:8 and 1 Timothy 1:15.

3. The Preachers' Burden Of His Faith

a. It is extremely trying for the Preacher to consistently attempt to instill faith in the hearts of Believers, when many times the Preacher's faith is severely lacking.
b. Every Preacher who has had a burden knows what it means to say and to pray, "Lord, I believe, but help thine my unbelief".
c. Look at John the Baptist and his burden of Faith (Matthew 11:1-3).

6. The "Ought To" Burden Of The Preacher.

A. There are certain general burdens every Preacher "ought to" have.

B. Every Preacher "ought to" have a burden for:
1. The Word - 2 Timothy 2:15, Matthew 22:29
2. Lost Souls - Mark 16:15, Acts 1:8
3. People - John 15:12, 1 John 4:20
4. Excellence - Daniel 5:12, Daniel 6:3, Philippians 4:14
5. Social Justice - Matthew 25: 34-40
6. The Lives of Young People - Matthew 19: 13-14, Ecclesiastes 12:1

Tommie E. Davis is a unique young minister who was born on June 30, 1964 at the Daughtery County Air Force Base Hospital in Albany, Georgia. Tommie and his mother, Delores S. Davis and his two brothers moved to Nashville and joined John Wesley Methodist Church. Tommie has received spiritual guidance and direction from the following men of God in Nashville: the late Dr. James T. Turner at New Hope Baptist Church, Dr. Michael L.

Graves, Sr. of The Temple Church. Tommie now serves diligently as an Associate Minister at Mt. Zion Baptist Church-Nashville under the Senior Pastor, Bishop Joseph W. Walker, III. Tommie plans to enroll in the Religious Studies program at Trevecca Nazarene University in Nashville, Tennessee in Spring, 2001. Minister Davis also serves as member of the Prince Hall Free & Accepted Masons, Capitol Hill Lodge #251.

MINISTER RODNEY K. DIGGS

"IS THERE A PHARAOH IN THE HOUSE?"

EXODUS 5:1-23

Everybody knows the story of Moses, left at the river in a basket, lived in Pharaoh's house, killed a man, had a speech problem, loved and obeyed God, led the Israelites out of Egypt and across the Red Sea. But, I want to focus on the antagonist in this passage, Pharaoh, King of Egypt and his important role then and now!

The Pharaoh in the book of Exodus was ruler over the largest empire known to man. To the Egyptians, Pharaoh means "Great House". This Pharaoh's given name was Rameses II, which lets us know that he was a second generation Pharaoh and had inherited his powerful position in a powerful country.

Pharaoh had clout because of his bloodline! Rameses II, King of Egypt ruled a country that held God's people in brutal bondage. Pharaoh ruled in a land that was polytheistic - meaning they served and worshiped many gods. As a matter of fact, Pharaoh and his people served nearly 80 different gods. Pharaoh was an oppressor of God's chosen people.

Is There A Pharaoh In Your House? Your Pharaoh could and might be your boss at work, your neighbor, a professor at school or maybe, even your spouse. Is there a Pharaoh in the House?

Your Faith Will Confuse Your Oppressor!

Afterward Moses and Aaron went to Pharaoh and said "This is what the Lord, the God of Israel, says: 'Let my people go,' so that they may hold a festival to me in the desert." Pharaoh said, "Who is the Lord, that I should obey him and let Israel go? I do not know the Lord and I will not let Israel go." Then they said, " The God of the Hebrews has met with us, Now let us take a three-day journey into the desert to offer sacrifices to the Lord our God, or he may strike us with plagues or with the sword." (Exodus 5:1-3)

Pharaoh knew of "other" gods, but did not know the God of Israel, the God of the Hebrews- Jehovah or Yahweh! Plus Pharaoh estimated the character and power of their god by the abject and miserable condition of the Israelites and concluded that "their god" ranked lowest of all gods. BIG MISTAKE!!!

Your Pharaoh's ignorance will lead to their own destruction! How can others believe and follow the God we serve, if we are enslaved to their gods, the god of money, the god of power, the god of position, the god of a great big house? Those are idle gods! The Bible states in Exodus 20:3, "You shall have no other god before me!"

But, this Pharaoh could not accept their God due to an "ism"- "Classism". The Egyptian Pharaohs believed in "classism" and customs. Because Pharaoh served many gods and none of his gods would ever ask him to move from a place of a great empire and comfort and go to a place of confusion and barrenness. To go to a wilderness, to go to a place where nothing makes sense. What's there? To go to a place that will take you three days by foot to reach, so you can have a feast, a festival in the desert? That doesn't make sense! Pharaoh must have thought, none of the eighty major gods he worshiped would ever ask that of him. That made no sense to him!! The Israelites faith in God confused him.

Pharaoh's custom was to honor the god of the river, the god of the land and the god of the sun, but not the god of the slaves! A Pharaoh wants us to serve their gods and will wonder out loud, What are you doing? Your Faith Will Confuse Your Oppressor!

Realize That Your Oppressor Has P.M.S.
(Pharaoh's Mean Spirit!)

P.M.S. is a medical condition directed by God! Pharaoh's actions were manufactured by the God of the Hebrews. You don't believe the first time preacher? Well turn to Exodus 9:12 "The Lord hardened Pharaoh's heart". Again, drop down to verse 35, "The heart of Pharaoh was hardened". One more time, for the truly skeptical. Go to Exodus 11:10 "Lord hardened Pharaoh's heart so that he would not let the children of Israel go".

Pharaoh was NOT in control of his own actions! God hardened his heart, not strengthened his heart. I am not a medical doctor, nor do I play one on television, so, I sought out a health care professional to give me some understanding of what physical symptoms Pharaoh must have been experiencing. I spoke to a good friend of mine, who happens to be a Clinical Nurse Specialist, she informed me that when hardening of the arteries of the heart takes place it causes poor circulation of the blood to the brain. With less blood to the brain, that causes a decrease of oxygen to the brain which causes impaired thinking, irrational thoughts and actions. Hmmm, sounds like anybody you know or have been around? Also, there is pain, immeasurable pain. When you are in pain, your thinking is not clear.

God hardened his heart, not strengthened his heart! God manipulated Pharaoh to serve God's purpose! All-powerful Pharaoh, King of the mighty empire of Egypt was used as a puppet by the God of the Hebrews. In short, Pharaoh got "Played"!

Bricks Without Straw

To show his contempt for God's people, Pharaoh called them lazy, lazy good for nothin' trifflin' kind of brothers and commanded them to make bricks without straw. Straw would not be given to them. They would have to search for the stubble themselves. And at the same time continue to meet their daily production. Bricks without Straw - Straw was the main substance in Egyptian brick. Bricks were used to build monuments, homes and the empire. They had to gather their own straw- the main substance. Substance equals Faith for the modern day Christian. Your Pharaoh has said to you, I don't understand what you're doing or the god you serve and you want to go off to some distant place from me. No you're not! As a matter of fact, I will no longer supply you with the main ingredient you need to perform your daily tasks - money, moral support, financial support, affection, faith or confidence in you. You will have to go and gather your own "substance"!

This makes me think about how my people, my ancestors, my Christian brothers and sisters are constantly forced to make bricks without straw. A few examples: You're admitted to college, but no financial aid is available, you're hired for a job, but because someone felt you were hired by a quota system, you were not given the budget or support you need, or take Metro Nashville school teachers, they're given students to teach, but in unsafe buildings with limited supplies and no increase in pay. Make Bricks Without Straw! And, historically black state supported universities (under a separated but equal edict) were only given 10% of their state allotment of funds, but were still expected to graduate scholars and great contributors - "Bricks" in this great empire called the United States of America. Bricks Without Straw! But, they have and continue to produce outstanding pillars in the community. Many of you may not know this, but the cell phone we heavily depend on everyday was developed by a graduate of Tennessee State University. A university that for decades was mandated by their Pharaoh to Make Bricks Without Straw!

My God, the God of the children of Israel provides and makes provision in spite of any Pharaoh. God will make a way somehow! Won't he? God will supply all my needs according to his riches and or in glory! If you trust in God, you won't be affected by "Pharaoh's Mean Spirit"!!!

Your Solution Is Here Among Us

Moses returned to the Lord and said, "O Lord, why have you brought trouble upon this people? Is this why you sent me? Ever since I went to Pharaoh to speak in your name, he has brought trouble upon this people, and you have not rescued your people at all."
(Exodus 5:22-23)

The last two verses make me want to shout! For right here, I discovered that if there is a Pharaoh in the house, then I know that there MUST be a Moses in the house!!!

You see, my God said He would supply all my needs according to His riches and or in glory! If there is a Pharaoh in your house or life, then there is a "Moses" here somewhere!!! Wherever there is a Pharaoh, God supplies a Moses! Oh, the name Moses means the same thing in Egyptian as it does in Hebrew: to draw out or to bring out.

Moses is called the deliverer by many Christians today, when in fact Moses did not deliver the Israelites out of bondage, IT WAS GOD! Think about it, when you "draw" water for a bath it's not the act of drawing the water that makes you clean, but the getting in and washing yourself with the soap. In the Christian's case, the water is the Word of God and the soap, well, the soap is the studying and living in God's will. God and only God will deliver you from your bondage. God will deliver you out of your Egypt. God will always provide you with a Moses to deal with your Pharaoh and draw you to Him.

The history of this country bears this out. When there was a Pharaoh, God provided Denmark Vessey - a Moses. Another Pharaoh, another Moses: Nat Turner, Marcus Garvey led some of our people out of this land and across an ocean, another Moses. One of my personal heroes, Harriet Tubman was certainly a Moses! To lead God's chosen people out of the bondage in the deep south. Talk about a three day journey for a feast, my God! How many rivers did she have to cross to get God's people to the promised land? God also whispered in the ear of another Moses by the name of Martin, Dr. Martin Luther King, Jr. Pharaoh was the Jim Crow Laws of the south. Dr. King "drew" us a picture of a better land. God supplied the Moses!

So, if there is a Pharaoh in your house, I know there is a

Moses in your house. If there is a Moses in your house draw close to the one who sent him. May God continue to bless You and keep you safe. This is my prayer. Amen.

Minister Rodney Diggs is the President and Co-Founder of One Flesh Ministries with his wife Minister Zenola Diggs. Minister Diggs is a native of Detroit and Battle Creek, Michigan and a graduate of the University of Michigan. Minister Diggs is currently pursuing a Masters of Divinity from David Lipscomb University in Nashville, Tennessee. Minister Diggs serves as Co-Overseer of Mt. Zion Baptist Church - Nashville's Marriage Ministry. He is the father of three sons, Cameron, K. Darren and Victor Diggs and has two granddaughters, Zion and Zayna. Minister Diggs is a Life Member of Kappa Alpha Psi Fraternity, Inc.

Minister John E. Girton, Jr.

"Re-Member the Body of Christ"

I Corinthians 12:1

"And now, brothers, I want to write about the special abilities the Holy Spirit gives to each of you, for I don't want any misunderstanding about them."

To one person the Spirit gives the abilities to give advice; someone else may be especially good at studying and teaching, and this is his or her gift from the same Spirit. He gives special faith to another, and to someone else the power to heal the sick. He gives power for doing miracles to some, and to others power to prophesy and preach. He gives someone else the power to know weather evil spirits and speaking through those who claim to be giving God's messages – or weather it is really the Spirit of God who is speaking. Still another person is able to speak in languages he or she never learned; and others, who do not know the language either, are given power to understand what is being uttered. It is the same Holy Spirit who gives all these gifts and power, deciding what each one of us should have.

It is then noteworthy that we are all gifted in some way. We all have a special place according to these things which are provided freely to us. This being the case, it is interesting to watch how we independently work in isolation of each other according to our gifts and our power. We function on islands as if what we do will ultimately affect us alone. We use our gifts when it benefits us and we don't use them when operating in them isn't beneficial to us.

But that is not the way God has made us. He has made many parts for our bodies and has put each part just where He wants it to be. What a strange thing the human body would be if it had only one part! So He has made many parts, but still there is only one body.

The eye can never say to the hand, "I do not need you." The head can never say to the foot, "I do not need you."

And some of the parts that seem weakest and least important are really very necessary. Yes, we are especially glad to have some parts that seem rather odd! And we carefully protect sensitive body parts like our eyes, those parts that are vital to us, while of course other extremities do not require this special care and protection. So, God has put the body together in such a way that extra honor and care are given to those parts that might otherwise seem less important. This makes for happiness among the parts, so that the parts have the same care for each other that they do for themselves. If one part suffers, all parts suffer with it, and if one part is honored, all parts are glad.

Background on the Situation
Corinth was an ancient and celebrated city of Greece, on the Isthmus of Corinth, and about forty miles west of Athens, Greece. A remarkable feature was the Acro Corinthus, a vast landing of rock which rose abruptly to the height of 2,000 feet about sea level. The summit or peak of this gigantic rock was so extensive that it once contained an entire town. Corinth was a place of great mental activity as well as of commercial and manufacturing enterprises. It is here were the stage was set for Paul's letters.

Why the Letter to the Corinthians?
St. Paul authored the first Epistle to the Corinthians after staying in the city of Corinth for a year and a half. Other teachers, lectures and prophets began speaking to the

people of Corinth shortly after Paul left the city. Now, Paul had surely worked hard and long setting up the church and instructing the members on the Gospels. However, as soon as he left, their minds began to flip flop. They were becoming confused due to the teachings of other false prophets. It is written how the members of the church at Corinth had become extravagantly wasteful, lacking self restraint. This city, once well respected for it's wealth of knowledge, had fallen victim to it's own immorality. Acts 19:1 describes how the church began to divide. The members had begun to fragment themselves into two, three, and even four separate factions. Other doctrines and false prophets desired to instruct the people in the total opposite of Paul's' teachings. And just before the church of Corinth had fallen into utterly disarrayed pieces, Paul picked up his pen and began to write. And as you will read, Paul's letters addressed a multitude of problems plaguing the Corinthians. All of which suppressed this once great city's ability to operate in it's full potential.

As we enter the first few verses of First Corinthians 12, we find that Paul opened this section using parallel statements to make his point.

The Living Bible reports:
You will remember that before you became Christians you went around from one idol to another, not one of which could speak a single word. But, now you are meeting people who claim to speak messages from the Spirit of God. How can you know whether they are really inspired by God or whether they are fakes? Here is the test; No one speaking by the power of the Spirit of God can curse Jesus, and no one can say "Jesus is Lord," and really mean it unless the Holy Spirit is helping him.

Now God gives us many kinds of special abilities, but it is

the same Holy Spirit who is the source of them all. There are different kinds of services to God, but it is the same Lord we are serving. There are many ways in which God works in our lives, but it is the same God who does the work in and through all of us who are His. The Holy Spirit displays God's power through each of us as a means of helping the entire church.

The Corinthians already knew that Christians did not have the same spiritual gifts. Although they knew this many did not like it. From there, Paul parallels diversity of gifts from the same spirit and differences of administration to the same Lord. So effective is this literary technique that Paul uses it, yet, one addition time, stating that there are diversities of operations and the same God which worketh all in all.

Knowing that these gifts from God are so diverse and plentiful, an example can be easily set. That example is that in the life of a Christian there is one organism, the body of Christ. The body of Christ is headed by one Chief Executive Officer, and this is God. God has set up His body to operate and function no differently than the body of you and I. In your body there is but one brain which guides the activities of one person, YOU! It is for this reason, no one can decide for you what will be your favorite color or what type of music you will like, nor what type of mate you will choose to marry. Those decisions are instinctly made by you for you.

This simple anthropomorphic example of the anatomy of the human existence was the tactic Paul chose to explain his point to the Corinthians. As we advance to the twelfth verse we notice how Paul is translating the physical body with the body of Christ.

Example of How These Gifts Work in the Body of Christ

Our bodies have many parts but the many parts make up only one body when they are all together. So it is with the "Body" of Christ. Each of us is a part of the body of Christ. Some of us are Jews, some are Gentiles, some are slaves and some are free. But the Holy Spirit has fitted us all together into one body. We have been baptized into Christ's body by the one spirit, and have all been given that same Holy Spirit.

Yes, the body has many parts, not just one part. What would the head of the body think if the foot says, "I am not a part of the body because I am not a hand." The difference between the two body parts does not make either of them any less a part of the body. And what would one think if you heard your ear say, "I'm not part of the body because I am only an ear, and not an eye?" Would that make it any less a part of the body? Suppose the whole body were an eye, then how would you hear? Or, if your whole body were just one big ear, how could you see?

However primitive society may have been over 1,939 years ago, enough was known about the humanity to make this distinct point; in order for your body to maximize it's potential, all of your parts must work together. In other words the members of your body must be in there proper place, doing what they were meant to do to bring glory to the body as a whole. It did not take an ancient brain surgeon to figure out that feet are no good for walking if your eyes can't see where to go. Just try walking out of your home today with your eyes closed. Conversations become difficult if you all of a sudden can't hear the words being spoken. Young people, the next time you're in class try plugging your ears and taking notes. The members of your bodies must be in their places doing what they were intended to do.

What would you look like walking around all day on your hands? The members of your body have a task to perform.

Have you ever dislocated a body part? A shoulder, or finger, knee or disc? It's hard to function when you can not move your entire arm after dislocating an elbow.

Some of you may know of a dislocated member in the body of Christ. Someone who is always in the wrong place at the wrong time doing the wrong thing. It is hard to make any progress when you have dislocated members. You know how hard it is to function with one dislocation. Now think of how hard it is when you have two, three, or even four dislocated members. It is painful when you have an out-of-socket member. This is what Paul and I are getting at.

When you become a member of the body of Christ, an obligation you must adhere to is that of Purpose. You must seek out your spiritual gift and begin to perform. When you decide to walk the road with Jesus, you have decided to "Get-in where you fit-in."

Neither the physical body nor the body of Christ can function unless all of the members or parts understand their God given spiritual purposes and gifts. You're directly related to your purpose.

You will find in Acts chapter 9 a dramatic example of an encounter with purpose. As many of you will recall Paul was not always the ecumenical icon that he is here in the 12th chapter of Corinthians. At one time his name was Saul, the Pharisee. Pharisees did everything they could to destroy the message and mission of Christ and anyone who followed the Christian doctrine. Saul was determined at one point to destroy every Christian. He had requested a letter addressed to synagogues in Damascus, requiring their cooperation in the persecution of any believers found there, both men and women, so that he could bring them in chains to Jerusalem.

However, God had intended this day to relocate Saul by revealing to him his purpose. That day on the Damascus road Saul came face to face with his God given purpose. That encounter on the road to Damascus changed Saul's life forever. Saul the Pharisee became Paul the Apostle.

Although your encounter does not need to be as dramatic as Paul's, you too need to discover the purpose God has created you for. You got to get-in where you fit-into God's plan.

Now the purpose of something is the reason for which it exists or, in other words, the manufacturer's original intent for making it. I do not know what God has created for you. I do not know what gifts God has planted in you. Thus, the purpose of a thing cannot be discovered by asking another thing. Paul would agree that if he were to ask one of his drinking buddies what his purpose was they may have said to kill all of the Jews. Likewise, if you were to ask a class mate or co-worker what they thought your purpose was they might say to graduate, get good grades or work enough overtime to make the maximum amount of money possible. If you went to the store to buy a vacuum and wanted to get a better idea of which one would serve you the best, you would not ask the vacuum for it's opinion of what it could do? Only the manufacturer of the equipment truly knows why the equipment was created and what features the equipment must have to do the job.

God is your source and manufacturer. He knows why He gave you life and endowed you with the personality, talents and ambitions that make you unique to the body of Christ. He wants you to discover why you were born so you can fulfill your purpose as a functioning member in the body of Christ. A sense of purpose gives life meaning. It moves you beyond existence to fulfilling a productive life.

Someone said that life without a purpose is an experiment. For some uncanny reason we as contemporary, intelligent, and technologically advanced human beings must spend our time on purposeless and unproductive living.

Do you know someone who wastes a lot of their time and yours doing things with no purpose in mind. Song writers use their talents to write songs that contribute to purposelessness. Why? Wasting time and talent producing a song that contributes to the sexual misconduct of human beings in the mist of non-curable disease serves no purpose. Why do our people continue to act as if life without purpose is the way to live?

Have you ever tried to accomplish a task only to find a purposeless individual in the way, stunting your very good intentions.

We must understand that every child is created with a purpose. Many of us simply never seem to discover our assignments. The 12th chapter of First Corinthians explains in verse 11 that when you were a child you spoke like a child, you understood as a child. But, when you became a man and when you became a woman, you put away childish things.

So, you ask what are you trying to say to me? I am saying that if you have not had an encounter with your maker or your manufacturer to find out your true meaning, your task, your satisfaction, your purpose, then it is time for you to accept the responsibilities of a grown up. I don't expect an 11 year old child to understand his or her purpose in life. I do however expect his or her parents to know. And at some point in all of our lives we must funnel through the rights of passages and accept some responsibilities. One of which is to begin to seek our purpose and chart a path to accomplish it.

How then do we take advantage of what Paul is saying to us a members on the body of Christ?

How then do we safeguard ourselves and our loved ones from manifesting unproductive behavior?

And most of all, how do we, who are unsure of our true purposes, identify our purpose within the realm of Christianity? Since we now know that only the Creator knows the purpose of a creation, then it is no wonder what initial steps are to be taken. We must go back to the mind of our manufacturer to find out the purpose for our existence. Nobody knows the product like the creator, no matter who the creator is. If you make a dress, no one knows that dress better than you. If you build a house, you know where you used old wood that nobody else can see because it is covered by paint.

You are related to where you came from. That means nobody knows you like the one from whom you came.

God who created you knows how He designed you t operate. God who created you knows how He designed yo to operate. He wants you to understand His thoughts towar you and His purpose for your life. If you try to live withou God you will, and probably already have, completely mes up your life, because life without purpose brings abou abuses.

Look around you. Many people have food, homes, cars friends, mothers, fathers and families that they are abusing They do not know the purpose of these people and things s they keep abusing them. If you do not know the spiritua gifts of a product, ask it's manufacturer. If you do not know the purpose of your family and friends, go to God Knowledge of purpose is the only way to avoid abuse.

It is time to find out our responsibilities to God. It is time t take some time and go off into our designated places to hav a long, introspective discussion with our maker. Some of u who have been feeling dissatisfaction with our lives need t stop and discover what type of member God wants us to be You can't ask me and you can't ask a friend. Once you hav discovered the type of member God wants you to be then it i time to relocate yourself in the body of Christ. It will then b time to realign yourself with your spiritual gifts and you membership status and begin to work as the instrument fo which you were intended. Do not live your life dislocated Do not waste your time without a purpose. Do not live a experiment, live a life. Live a life full of the advantage offered by God. And young people, understand that ther will come a day when you, too, will want to consider yoursel grown. At that time you will need to do one very importan thing. Go to God and seek your purpose in life. For some i will be obvious and for others it may take a day, a week, or year(s). God has to send you by some people. All of whic will offer you a few pieces to life's puzzle.

Re-Member the Body of Christ. Be a responsible member i the Body of Christ.

Reverend John E. Girton, Jr.

The Reverend John E. Girton, Jr. has been in and around the Christian experience all of his life. A native of Indianapolis, Indiana and the son of a baptist minister, his personal and professional foundation was molded around biblical principles and Christian values.

Although hearing one's own father preach each Sunday serves the need for a role model, it was very easy to dismiss much of what was being taught or preached due to familiarity; he simply heard it before. Little did he know that those biblical pearls would be the building blocks for his present psych.

As early as age thirteen, John began developing his God given talents in the television and radio industry. By age eighteen he was selected as the youngest and only African American cameraman during the 1987 Pan Am Games in Indianapolis, Indiana. Before his twenty first birthday he had produced an anti-drug, crime and violence music video which aired in regular rotation on Black Entertainment Television (BET). By the time John earned his B.S. degree in communications from Ball State University he had already accumulated numerous awards, working for companies such as CBS Sports, BET's Video Soul Live, and as the Producer/Director of the Bea Motten Foster daily talk show.

In 1993 John accepted the call of ministry. He felt chosen to provide spiritual as well as professional leadership long before realizing what this would actually mean for his life. Throughout all of his personal accomplishments, John constantly felt the agony of a society groping for sound, Christian standards in a contemporary age.

As John puts it, "Being a young African American man, I know the demands for positive and effective leadership are great. In the Christian community these demands intensify and are vital to the future of our families, communities, nation and world."

In early 1993 John began traveling the world as a concert tour manager for the popular recording group "High Five." Two years later he moved to Chicago, Illinois to continue his career as a graphic designer for companies such as J. Walter Thompson, Walgreen's, Sigma Gamma Rho Sorority, Inc. and the 7-up Corporation. He was later hired as the first African American designer for David C. Cook Publishing, the largest distributor of Christian education literature in the world.

Upon relocating to Colorado Springs, Colorado in 1995, John was hired as the Artist Relations Manager for Compassion International, an International Christian child development organization. A few months later he was promoted to Compassion USA's National Marketing Manager, servicing the marketing needs of Christian child development programs across the United States.

Two years later, the now married Girton's relocated to Nashville, Tennessee to focus their attention on the couples four year old business. Within one year Mass Media, LLC, the couples creative services agency, had not only taken the leap from part-time to full-time operation, they also landed several major projects including the development of the Bobby Jones Gospel image, Fisk Universities Race Relations Institute program designs, and developing the corporate image for the Mt. Zion Baptist Church of Nashville. Mass Media was also accepted into the Tennessee State University-Nashville Incubation Center where they are now experiencing tremendous growth in the religious and secular markets. Clients include the Emmanuel Baptist Church of Colorado Springs, Colorado, Loving Baptist Church of Indianapolis, Indiana and West Point Baptist Church of Chicago, Illinois.

A life of growth and prosperity of this magnitude can be attributed only to God's will for the lives of John and his wife La Wanda. No matter what projects or proposals they enter, their goals are to first uplift the kingdom. In his professional and personal life John wishes for nothing else but to point others toward the cross.

"The scripture reads, 'The harvest is plenteous and the laborers are few. Therefore, pray the Lord of the harvest to send out laborers into His harvest' Matthew 9:37 This is the task God placed upon my heart, one that I am encouraged to maintain."

John is married to La Wanda C. L. Girton and the two have one daughter, Faith Janez Girton. They reside in Nashville, Tennessee.

Photo's are available via e-mail.
Request to: **biophoto@massmedia.org**

Minister William C. Haynes

Forgiving 101: A Lesson From The Cross

"Then Jesus said, Father, forgive them; for they know not what they do." (Luke 23:34(a)

Jesus Christ was (and is) the Master Teacher. Even from the cross He taught a powerful lesson on forgiveness. It is very important that we understand forgiveness. Forgiveness is tied to every Christian thought or concept we can imagine. Our hope, our joy, our love, our peace, all are impacted by whether or not we are able to forgive others. Jesus taught that if we forgive others their trespasses, God will forgive us for our sins and conversely, if we don't forgive others, God won't forgive us. And if God doesn't forgive us, we have no salvation. The salvation we have is because of God's grace and mercy towards us. And certainly we have done nothing to deserve grace or mercy. It's only because we have a forgiving God that we receive either.

There is so much to consider when it comes to forgiveness. We could ponder Jesus healing sickness by forgiving. You remember the man with the palsy who was lowered through the roof. Did not Jesus heal him by saying "Man thy sins are forgiven thee"? Or we could think about Jesus practicing what He preached, that even as He was dying He was forgiving folks. But what God wants you to know through this sermon is that if you have an unforgiving spirit, then you have blessings that are being blocked, prayers that are not being responded to, help that is not forthcoming.

Many don't forgive because they simply don't know what is involved. Well from the cross Jesus offers some very basic elements to forgiveness. Let's look at the Word of God. First, let's look at when to forgive. The Bible says, "THEN JESUS SAID ....", The word 'then' suggests to me a specific point in time. So I asked, what point in time? Well if you look at verse 33, the Bible says, "THERE THEY CRUCIFIED HIM". At first I was confused, because I wanted to know how He could speak if He had already been crucified. But what I found out through further study is that to crucify is not to merely put to death .

Crucifixion is actually a process of torture. One of the definitions in Webster's Dictionary for crucify is to persecute or torment. So what that says to me is that even as Jesus was in the midst of His tribulation, even as He was being persecuted and tormented, He forgave. He didn't wait until later, as many of us do, after we've had time to think about it or cool down or wait for an apology. No, He forgave as He was being wronged.

Which brings me to where we should forgive. The Bible says "THERE THEY CRUCIFIED HIM" (verse 33) and "THEN JESUS SAID" (verse 34). Now we know that Jesus didn't come down from the cross. That means He forgave from where He was being wronged. So not only did He forgive during His torment, He forgave in the midst of His tormentors.

And think about it, if anyone could have afforded to wait, it was Jesus. He could have just gone to His borrowed tomb to think it over for about three days. After all, He knew that even though He was being put to death, that He was coming back. Or He could have waited until His second coming, He is coming back you know. But Jesus didn't wait, because He knew that if He didn't forgive then and there, His victory would not be complete, that He would not have done what He set out to do. And you need to understand that if you don't learn to forgive, your victory can't be complete either.

Now let me show you how Jesus forgave. The Bible says "THEN JESUS SAID, FATHER FORGIVE THEM" - in other words, He prayed. You have to understand that prayer is conversation with the Father. Jesus was 100% God, but He was also 100% man. And we saw in the Garden of Gethsemane that the flesh, the man, was not anxious to go to the cross. Well I can imagine that from the cross, the flesh was not as willing to forgive either. Jesus knew that the human part of Him did not really have the capacity to forgive, but aren't we thankful He knew to go to the Father. In that moment Jesus showed us the process of forgiveness: 1) recognize you've been done wrong; 2) give it to the Father; 3) then leave it alone.

We've all heard it said that prayer changes things. I want you to notice something. Jesus prayed, but it did not change His immediate situation, but His prayer did save the world. It may not look like God is changing your situation when you pray, but if you pray in faith, in the spirit, your prayer will change your world.

While we're at this point in the text, I want you to see who Jesus forgave. "THEN JESUS SAID, FATHER FORGIVE THEM." Now common sense tells us that everyone in the crowd did not play an equal part in the crucifixion. But Jesus didn't ask for forgiveness for those who had only laughed or made fun of Him, those who did less serious things. No, He asked for forgiveness for them, all of them. You need to understand that you can't pick and choose who you forgive. You can't forgive just the person who spilled something on your new silk blouse or who stepped on your foot as they were taking a seat on your pew, but you've got to forgive the spouse who walked out on you and the kids. And you've got to forgive the one who enticed your spouse and convinced them to leave. You've got to forgive the one who beat on your sister or the one who shot your baby brother. You don't get the luxury of picking whom to forgive.

Finally I want you to see, why Jesus forgave. "THEN JESUS SAID, FATHER FORGIVE THEM; FOR THEY KNOW NOT WHAT THEY DO." Jesus knew that the crowd did not realize exactly who they were crucifying, even though they knew of the miracles and had heard the teaching. But He also knew that if He didn't forgive them, there would be no remission of sin and that was why He came to earth in the first place. He forgave because He was the Christ and He had no other choice. He knew that if He didn't forgive, the world would not be able to stand up under the wrath of God. And you must realize that the people who do you wrong don't know who you are either. They don't understand that you're a royal priesthood, a chosen generation. Understand that the folks who do you wrong don't know that in the Old Testament, God wiped out whole nations for coming against His chosen people. So as one who is Christ-like (that's what a Christian is you know), you have an obligation to forgive others to keep them from being destroyed because they are messing with God's elect.

One last thing. Jesus knew they didn't know what they were doing, because they didn't know exactly who He was, but Jesus knew who He was. And even though He was being put to death, He knew also that He would be returning to heaven to be with His Father, so He wasn't the one experiencing a problem. And you need to know who you are. Not that I would elevate you to the level of the Christ, but in the eighth chapter of Romans we are told that those who are led by the Spirit of God are the sons of God (isn't that who Jesus is, the Son of God?), and if children of God, joint heirs with Christ. That means that everything that Jesus is entitled to in heaven, so too are we. Everything Jesus can have, we can have. But the Bible goes on to say that if we want to be glorified together with Jesus, we must suffer with Him also. Just as Jesus suffered for the sins of the world, so too will you suffer in your Christian walk, often at the hands of others. But just like Jesus, you're not really the one with the problem, because you already know you have an eternal home with the Father. In the midst of His suffering Jesus forgave. Can you?

Minister William C. Haynes

William Haynes is a native of West Tennessee, born in Paris and raised in Jackson. He was educated in the Jackson public school system. He received two degrees from Tennessee State University in Nashville, a Bachelors of Science in Government and Public Affairs and a Master's of Public Administration. He has served in management for several agencies in Tennessee state government. Though it was not an intended career path, his major area of expertise is advocacy for children and families.

While growing up in Jackson, young William was a faithful member of the Macedonia Baptist Church. As many do, he strayed away from the church during his early adult years. However, as always, God's Word has proven to be true (train up a child in the way he should go and when he is old, he will not depart from it). William united with the Mt. Zion Baptist Church of Nashville in February 1997. His intention was to become a faithful member ready to serve in whatever capacity he might be needed, but God had other plans. In January 1998 William accepted God's call to the ministry.

Minister Haynes is married to Jacqueline, also a licensed minister. They have three children, Rosalind, Kellen and Kia. They are also foster parents and the "adoptive" parents of children too numerous to count.

Minister Reginald Hill

"God Did It To Finish It!"

(Exodus 14)

Chapter fourteen of this book takes place after the Israelites had been set free from Egypt. At the beginning of this chapter we see God giving Moses instructions to give to the Israelites. Here we see God strategically placing the Israelites in position because although, they look free there was still the threat of captivity. So God says hold up, wait a minute go back and because I am a Sovereign power and an all knowing God place yourselves in a position to leave nothing undone. Oh yes, sometime God will place us in a position that is not too comfortable, and looks strange to the enemy yet, He is a God that leaves nothing undone. Moses and the Israelites were obedient to what God had told them to do, but right at verses ten after leaving Egypt victoriously we see fear set in at the sight of the enemy. At that moment the Israelites were blinded and confused crying out to God for help, but hurting agents the man that God was using to help. All they wanted now was a way out of the situation they were in. Make no mistake my brothers and sisters fear will make you do some crazy things.

We must realize that God will place us in some situations in life that will make our enemies think we are defeated, but it's a different kind of set up. We must begin to look beyond the situation, look beyond that thing that you think is stifling your progress. Look beyond that husband or that wife that's treating you less than a child of God. Look beyond that brother or sister that wants to scandalize your name. Look beyond that supervisor or CEO that continually gives you a hard time.

Simply look beyond and then ask God what is your purpose here God, and what would you have me to do. I am convinced that if many of us would go beyond the surface of our situations we would realize it's not about us but it's all about God. Just as the children of Israel learned at their point of no return. They could not go around it, or walk away from it. They could only stand still, and see the salvation of the Lord.

What is God trying to salvage you from in your life today? Have you allowed God to put a pillar of cloud behind you and a pathway of deliverance before you just as he did for the children of Israel? God instructed Moses to lift up his rod and stretch forth his hand, at which time God made provision for the children of Israel to go forward from a bad situation. And because nothing would be left undone God also destroyed their enemies.

We must ask ourselves, in this situation, what does God what destroyed? That your people may see your salvation, and like Moses and the children of Israel we must become the willing vessel to be used by God. In every situation look to find the God factor (will God get the glory) and then at your point of no return when the hounds of hell are nipping at your ankles be encouraged.

Pick up your rod (which is the Word of God) stretch forth your hand proclaiming Joshua 1:5. "There shall not any man be able to stand before thee all the days of thy life: as I was with Moses, so I will be with thee: I will not fail thee, nor forsake thee". And then stand still and see the salvation of our Lord in your situation. My brothers and sisters God will provide a way for you to go forward. He will destroy that thing that is keeping you in bondage because; that situation that God has arranged you in, or

allowed
you to endure in. He's doing it, to finish it.

To God be the glory

With Love,
Minister Reginald Hill

Minister Reginald Hill was born in Cleveland Ohio, to Mrs. Claudia Hill and Author Ross, where he spent most of his childhood. He attended Tennessee State University where he received a Bachelor of Science degree in Sociology, and a Master of Education degree in Special Education. Minister Hill currently teaches in the Metro Nashville public school system. He was licensed in the exhortation ministry on August 13, 1999, by the Mt. Zion Baptist Church and Pastor Joseph W. Walker III. He is presently exercising God given gifts in the prison ministry at Mt. Zion, and working as chaplain with Priority Hospice Inc. Ministering the inspiring Word of God to those who are terminally ill. Minister Hill strongly believes that in all things we must seek the face of our God, for it is not by might or power, but by the Spirit of the Lord of hosts that we do all things.

May God's word continue to reveal His good pleasure for life! The blood is what his hands cover in my life!

Elder Donald R. Hutchinson, Jr.

"BLOOD ON HIS HANDS"

(Ezekiel 33:1-7)

In my hands, I hold the key to life and death, the key to eternity and damnation; in my hands, I hold the description of heaven and hell. Sixty-six books of love, lust; peace and punishment; joy and judgment; righteousness and wickedness; wisdom and foolishness; in my hands I hold the law; mercy; and even grace, the beginning and the end every Alleluia and Amen. In my hands I hold blessings and curses; instructions and ignorance. However perhaps one of if not the most important item in this book is the blood.

More important than tithing, counseling, worship, praise, and even prayer, the blood is the most important item in this book. Yes it has prophets, apostles, pastors, evangelists, and even teachers; sacrifices, healings, hope, confidence, covenants, patience and promises, but the source, the essence, principle foundation, every precept, statute, commandment, and office, every answer to every question; even life itself is the blood. This book called the Bible, the written voice of God, is different things to different people, it is judgment to the unsaved, redemption to the saved, a new beginning to the backslider, the truth to every cheat, liar and deceiver, and a bridle to the tongue of every backbiter and gossiper, this book this simple book to some but the blood book to me. This book, this bloody book is correction to the disobedient, wisdom to the prudent, direction to the lost. These simple pages, chapters like any other chapters, words like any other words, the punctuations, quotations, phrases, sentences are like any other grammatical syntax, but when bound together, brought forward, and the blood applied these same words become alive these same words these bloody words can make a drunk man sober, a drug addict clean, a homosexual straight, a fornicator abstain, a rebellious church evangelize all from this book, these words, the blood, in my hand. In this blood book you will find a) forgiveness, b) repentance, c) protection, in these very chapters you will find d) longsuffering, e) fulfillment, f) righteousness, and g) faithfulness.

In this book, well we cannot look at every verse, chapter nor book, but let us look at Ezekiel this priest, this prophet, this son of man, and this watchman over Israel. Now to understand the passage and why, where, when, what, and how it applies to our lives we must look at the passage in it proper context. We cannot pick out any verse and begin to live because with every step there is a process, for the Psalmist wrote that "The steps of a good man are ordered by the Lord: and he delighteth in his way." So let us look at the condition and the reason for Ezekiel and his prophetic word.

1. Now the first thing we need to write down is the God never sends his word without a reason and for a condition. One writer wrote "So shall my word be that goeth forth out of my mouth: it shall not return unto me void, but it shall accomplish that which I please, and it shall prosper in the thing whereto I sent it." Therefore, God never sends the word without a reason and for a condition. Now the reason is clear but the condition is not as clear as we could hope. God is sending his word to the children of Israel to warn them from impending danger. God sends his word to instruct the children of Israel to recognize the warning and respond accordingly. And does not God do the same today whenever we attempt to do wrong God sends his word in an attempt to keep us from hurting ourselves. See during the days of Israel God would only speak through a select group of men and women, he spoke to them through Abraham, he spoke to them through Noah, he spoke to them through Jacob, he spoke to them through Moses and through Moses God not only spoke but also wrote it down. God not only speaks through his servants but also through his written word. You know the story how God gave Moses the tablets in the mountain and after they were destroyed; He gave him the second tablets in which he placed in the ark, which was inside the tabernacle. This is a testimony to any church that in order to build correctly the church must be built upon the word of God which should be placed upon the hearts of the people, therefore this building is built to house the hearts of the people that are filled with the word of God, any other way is unprofitable and dung. Nevertheless, we see that even this was not enough, and because of Israel's disobedience, Ezekiel is made a watchman over them. The people no longer appreciated God neither respected his commandments so as a result of their disobedience God allows them to be taken captive and here we find Ezekiel giving them words of warning.

2. Which leads to our second point, God never sends his word without warning or consequence. Ezekiel warns of impending destruction and consequences for the obedient and disobedient. However, the people could not understand why now, what consequence, what possibly could be any worse than what they were already in. What else guilt could bring them any lower than where they are now, stripped of their dignity, their peace, their possessions, their position, and even the presence of God. Like so many of you who are looking at your life and asking how can it get any worse and just like Israel God is sending his word for you to take your eyes off your tangible items but rather your intangible, Israel had yet to realize that their deliverance was in the warning.

3. Here is our last point; God never sends his word without a way out. Israel was on the verge of losing their relationship with God, their protection form God, their anointing of God. Moreover, here in this word of warning God is speaking to each individual, where he is concerned about the intangible more than the tangible. Now do not misunderstand me God desires for all of us to be successful, to be clothed, sheltered, and nurtured, but God more importantly desires a sincere and consistent relationship with each one of you. Not just for you to be happy but have joy, not just well but delivered, not just succeeding but overcoming, not just alright but whole, not just struggling but established and here within this word, this warning that God has provided a way out.

Through this son of man, God places the responsibility but his word is just a warning but not a covering. Ezekiel being a man could not fulfill the law of sacrifice because the sacrifice had to be without blemish for here the Psalmist says, "Behold I was shapen in iniquity and in sin did my mother conceive me", remember God never sends his word without a way out. He we see Ezekiel, this priest, this prophet, this watchman, this first son of man, only a warning but not a way out but thanks be to God there was another son a second son of man, a second Adam, a second Moses, a second Solomon, a second Elijah, a second Jonah, a second word, this man Jesus Christ for one writer wrote "In the beginning was the word and the word was with God and the word was God. The same was in the beginning with God." And down in verse 14 "The word was made flesh and dwelt among us (and we beheld his glory, the glory as the only begotten of the Father) full of grace and truth." Jesus, the son of God; Jesus, the son of David; Jesus, the son of man; Jesus the son of righteousness; Jesus, the word of God, the accomplishing prospering whereto word. Pastor it is astonishing how we have no enthusiasm about Calvary, no love for his sacrifice, no joy for his victory, no praise for his triumph at Calvary, one song writer said "Years I spent in vanity and pride, Caring not my Lord was crucified knowing it was for me He died at Calvary" At Calvary is where you will find forgiveness, at Calvary you will find repentance, at Calvary you will find protection, at Calvary you will find longsuffering, at Calvary you will find fulfillment, at Calvary you will find righteousness, at Calvary you will find faithfulness, but most of all at Calvary you will find the blood, the bloody word, Jesus Christ, but just in case you can't get to Calvary just follow the trail, blood in the courtyard (where they beat and bruise for our iniquity), blood in the whipping post (where by his stripes we are healed), blood on the streets (where he bore our grief and carried our sorrows), blood on the cross (where he placed the chastisement of our peace), blood on the back of a merchant (where lay on him the iniquity of straying sheep), blood on the foot of the cross (where he was oppressed and afflicted for our sakes). Blood on his hands to redeem us back to God, blood on his feet to cover the footsteps of all sin, blood on his head to remind God of the sacrifice, blood on his side to remind us of his cleansing power. One songwriter penned, "What can wash away my sin. Nothing but the blood of Jesus. What can make me whole again. Nothing but the blood of Jesus. Oh how precious is that flow that makes me white as snow, no other friend I know. Nothing but the blood of Jesus." See this blood book from Genesis to Revelations, this blood was an offering in Genesis, a releasing in Exodus, a sacrifice in Leviticus, a covering in Numbers, an innocence in Deuteronomy, avenging in Joshua, this same blood of Jesus Christ is merciful in I Sam; reproving in II Sam.; revealing in Jeremiah; judgment in Ezekiel; promising in Zechariah; righteous in Matthew, healing in Mark; a testament in Luke; resurrecting in John; purchasing in Acts; justifying in Romans; adjoining in Corinthians; redemptive in Ephesus; peaceable in Colossians; everlasting in Hebrews; precious in Peter, agreeable in John; and cleansing in Revelations. The blood on the cross, the blood on the ground, the blood in the graveyard, the blood in the tomb, blood in the grave, life in the grave, the word in the grave, the reason in the grave, the warning in the grave, the way out in the grave, but early, early Sunday morning he got up, step out over everlasting and glory but didn't come empty handed for the Bible says "I am he that liveth, and was dead and behold, I am alive forever more, Amen; and have the keys of hell and of death." He got up. He got up. He got up. He ascended up. He ascended up and now sits on the right hand of the Father. All for the blood on his hands.

Minister Bernard Johnson

"Disconnected Because of Disobedience"

(Malachi 2:1-9)

Malachi is written during hard times when the priests of Israel have failed to recognize God as a high, honorable being. The priests of God bring disgrace upon the name of the Lord. They have failed to give God their best through sacrifices. Here, Malachi calls the "spiritually complacent" to a renewed relationship with God. In verse 2:1, God isn't talking to just pastors and preachers. We do know that all of us are priests. In 1 Peter 2:9, it reads, "But ye are a chosen generation, a royal priesthood, a holy nation, a peculiar people, that ye should show forth the praises of him who hath called you out of darkness into his marvelous light." Yet, we forget to show Him praise. We forget to call out the darkness so that it may be exposed and removed in the light. We fail to call out our dark side, so it may be exposed and removed in the light of God. God tells the priests, "...if you will not hear, and if ye will not lay it to heart, to give glory unto my name, I will even send a curse upon you, and I will curse your blessings." Like a tree that bears fruit on one day, and then withers on the next day. God will dry up your rushing river overnight.

1) It is very important that we hear God. Verse 2 reads, "If you do not listen, and if you do not set your heart to honor my name," says the Lord Almighty, "I will send a curse upon you, and I will curse your blessings. Yes, I have already cursed them, because you have not set your heart to honor me." What does God mean by hear? I remember when I was a child and my mother would call me and ask me a question or she would tell me to do something, and then she would ask if I could hear her. She didn't really want to know if I could physically hear her voice through the house, she wanted to know if I was listening to her, and if I was obeying her command. Here in verse 2, hear means to listen and obey. God is saying that if we fail to listen to Him, fail to set our heart and minds on Him, and fail to give Him praise, we shall be cursed. And these curses start with the blessings he has already given us. Just imagine that you're standing in your two- car garage and your BMW and Expedition turn into a bike and a cart right before your eyes. It may be brand new and it still has the new smell to it, but it will not start. Your new three story home has no power, every bathroom has a leak, and the A/C refuses to work. Your blessing may not be taken but they will be cursed.

2) Our personal disobedience has generational damage. Verse 3 reads, "Behold, I will corrupt your seed and spread dung upon your faces, even the dung of your solemn feasts; and one shall take you away with it." The seed mentioned here is our children. Think about the things your children will have to face because of your disobedience. There are enough things in the world for the children to worry about without them worrying about something in our past that may have an effect on them. We have a problem with tithing. We have a problem with coming to church on time. We have a problem with letting go of worldly things. Now think about this. Would you have a problem with all these things knowing that they will be a burden on your children? Think about the public embarrassment you would face simply because of disobedience. Here you are sitting on top of the world with a new job that has a six- figure salary attached, then the company files bankruptcy. Just imagine as you are taking out the trash, a hand comes down out of the heavens and places you on top of the trash heap. Instead of taking the trash out, you're taken out with the trash.

You may be wondering how the people of God were being disobedient. Verses 6-7 tells how Levi was obedient to God. It reads, "True instruction was in his mouth and nothing false was found on his lips. He walked with me in peace and uprightness, and turned many from sin. For the lips of a priest ought to preserve knowledge, and from his mouth men should seek instruction-because he is the messenger of the Lord Almighty. The priests did not honor, revere, respect, or worship God. They would build their own house up before giving to God's house. These are the priests of their time....not the followers. The priests gave false teachings. Somehow in between Genesis and Revelations, the preacher adds the book of Jackson or may take out the book of Psalms. This book speaks to those priests who have failed to teach God's word correctly, failed to stay upright with God, and failed to lead others away from sin. How can I help my brother with his problem of drinking and I'm known by face at University Liquors? How can I help my brother with sexual urges, and everyday I'm getting to know some young lady the way that Abraham knew Sarah? It goes on to say in verse 9, "So I have caused you to be despised and humiliated before all the people, because you have not followed my ways but have shown partiality in matters in the law". If you can not do God's business in a Godly fashion, you will be pointed out, picked up, removed, and replaced. But there is hope. There is a cure. There is a balm in Gilead. God provides His Son Jesus to execute His plan and gift of faith and justification known as grace. (God's Riches At Christ's Expense) Its all because of God's grace that we are not disconnected from his love and abundance. We fail to humble ourselves so that we may do God's will by loving and serving others the way that He loves and serves us.

Three steps that will save you from long term self inflicted trials and griefs:
1) Detect - Take an inward look at yourself being honest and realize what the problem is inside of you.
2) Correct-Correct the things within you by praying to God and being lead by His word.
3) Elect-Make a conscious effort and elect or choose to continue from the place that you had to leave to correct your problem. Don't sit in self-denial or guilt so it may build up within you and give death to things that God told you that there would be life. Remember that God gave you grace.

My car is a beautiful thing, not because of anything special, but because it goes when I need it to go. I remember a year or so ago my car would not start. But when I tried to start it, it sounded like it wanted to start but didn't have enough power, so I started using a portable jump starter. It had 900 cold cranking amps of power and could jump-start an 18-wheeler if it need it to and it worked well for awhile, but it was a temporary solution. It wasn't a cure. It was more of a prescription. So I sent it to a mechanic to detect a problem in the electrical system, because I could tell it was more of a power problem.

A day or so later, the mechanic tells me that the engine was not grounded. It simply wasn't grounded so all the power that the alternator made while it was running may have been used but it would always leak because it wasn't grounded. So he corrects the problem by grounding the engine. Many of you have been going through trials and you don't know what is going on. There may be a leak in your power system or you may be using something to give yourself a temporary power boost, but if you would just FIRMLY GROUND yourself in the WORD of GOD, you wouldn't lose any power, but it would only increase with the time that you are grounded. Remember when you lose your grounding, you lose the power of God.

Minister Bernard Johnson

Born April 16, 1977 early one Saturday morning, Bernard Johnson gave his life to God in the Fall of 1993 and was baptized in the name of the Father, the Son and the Holy Ghost at Rising Star Baptist Church in Birmingham, Alabama. In the fall of 1995, Bernard entered Tennessee State University in Nashville as a freshman to major in Electrical Engineering. Minister Johnson joined Mt. Zion Baptist Church - Nashville in 1996 under watchcare. As he continued his matriculation at Tennessee State University, he continued to feel God pulling at his heart. In the Spring of 1998, he accepted his calling as a teacher, preacher and exhorter of the Gospel of Jesus Christ.

Minister Sam Koya

"Consolidate, Evangelize, Conquer"

"Go into all the world and preach the gospel to every creature." This was the mandate given by our Lord Jesus Christ to His followers just before He stepped out of history back into eternity and glory. "Go and preach the gospel" was the order and it served as a seamless commission to all Disciples of Christ everywhere. The adherence of all Christians to this Great Commission through the ages has fallen far short of the vision and will of our Master.

A critical appraisal of the Church's stewardship to the Commission so far reveals a dismal picture of lackluster performance. Granted, the Church has grown phenomenally since the departure of Christ and the subsequent arrival of the Holy Spirit. But by no means has the Church's real growth potential been exploited aggressively and faithfully in accordance with the vision and power of our Master Jesus. He who gave the commission is of infinite potential and so is His Kingdom, the Church. The ability of the Church to make disciples of all nations and every creature is without any doubt real and boundless, given the fact that our Lord Jesus Christ heads the Church. So why are all nations and every creature in "all the world" not yet Disciples of Christ?

Speaking theoretically, it is possible to make disciples of all nations and every creature, realistically, this will not be. This is because, as we know, Salvation is for whosoever will. Sadly, not everyone will. This, however, does not take up all the slack between what ought to be-the disciple making of every nation and creature-and what is. Thus it must be that the Church is in partial default of the Master's commission. Clearly, the Church needs to shake itself out of its reverie, halt its perpetual slide into half-baked relevancy and near-total redundancy, and aggressively pursue the commission of the Master Jesus.

Shame and defeat seems to be hanging around the neck of the Church in place of the Cross and Victory. The Principalities and Powers seem to be prevailing against the Church on the battlegrounds of our communities, torturing and making captives of souls through drugs, alcohol, abject poverty, prostitution, crime, diseases and other sundry ills. Souls are being dispatched to hell in rapid-fire succession through murders, skewed abortions, and AIDS. Our Youth turn guns on each other, before our very eyes transforming into monsters of mass murder. Demons are making disciples of our children because the Church has shirked its responsibility of extending the answer to the misery of these mixed-up youngsters who have so many questions, but wrong answers. Homelessness, loneliness, illness, pain, suffering and hunger encamp in communities around our churches. Where is the pride of the Church in all this? Where is the victory of the Cross? What legitimacy can the Church lay hold to for its presence in our communities if its impact is not felt reverberatingly amidst the misery and ruins of socio-moral decadence? How long will the Church content itself with remaining a mere symbol of hope-a literal oasis, stagnant and inactive in a vast social desert laid bare of righteousness, peace and prosperity? How long will churches continue to remain glorified monuments of spiritual ineptitude in their surroundings? Beyond the occasional and ceremonial outreach days, what sustained efforts are churches making to feed the hungry, clothe the naked, shelter the homeless, heal the sick, and deliver captives from the kingdom of darkness? Enough of this shame! It is an eyesore to God. We Christians have taken hypocrisy to a higher level. In our fashionable and elegant Sunday best, we head to worship in the cocoon of our sleek cars, gliding blithely past human images of misery, pain, heartache, poverty and torment and yet hold our head high. There is something terribly wrong with this picture. God is very unhappy and thoroughly displeased with this diabolical hypocrisy. Are we not supposed to be the salt that seasons the earth? Where is our flavor? Our Master gave the Great Commission, Go bear my message of hope to all the earth. This is not an appeal. This is an order. Brethren, there is an element of urgency bearing on us all to faithfully heed this Commission lest the Master says to us on that Day "...for I was hungry and you gave Me no food, I was thirsty you gave Me no drink. I was a stranger and you did not take Me in, naked and you did not clothe Me, sick and in prison and you did not visit Me..."

There is work to be done-and urgently too!

We Christians may be too ensconced in the comfort of our various material blessings to feel the pain of lost and tortured souls in our neighborhoods. We may be too immune to empathize with the excruciating agony they go through every minute of their lives. Somewhere there is some hungry soul who does not know where their next meal is coming from; somewhere some poor innocent kid is being subjected daily to excruciating abuse by some drug-addicted parent, somewhere right now somebody is getting killed in a drive-by.... How can we call ourselves Christians and pretend we can't do anything? Should we not roll up our sleeves and go to work earnestly in spreading the news of hope to these tormented souls? Are we too uppity to invade our neighborhoods with the gospel of our Master? Are we too "upper classed" to get our hands dirty in the neighborhoods, evangelizing the under-privileged, the dis-privileged and the lost? God is telling each and every congregation, each and every Christian in Nashville, "...inasmuch as you did not do it to one of the least of these, you did not do it to Me."

This is a challenge from God. He is calling on us not to get complacent within the comfortable confines of our church buildings but to go out to the lost souls, preaching to them the Kingdom of God, healing the sick, cleansing the unclean, casting out demons and bringing deliverance to the oppressed. He is reminding us that this is our fundamental calling as Christians and this is where we need to re-direct our focus to. This call is especially strident and compelling on Pastors. God says you must not lose sight of the bottom line--- soul winning. Yes, your duty is to keep (feed, nurture) the flock but you must not get comfortable in the comfort zone of 'keeping'. With alertness and alacrity you must keep a keen eye on the work zone of 'winning'. You are mandated to keep winning the flock you are going to keep keeping. You are the Joshuas of today. Not only are you to keep the flock, you are to lead them to posses the land that belonged to them from before the foundation of the world. Our communities, schools, businesses, government etc....all belong to us. This is our promised inheritance. You must not let your God-given assignment be distorted or your focus distracted by the daily exigencies of church management, congregational control, socio-political or cultural interests, (all which are 'noises' that can pollute, constrict or contaminate the sacrosanct sanctity of your sacred mandate).

It is high time that Pastors realize that they must

precipitate and perpetuate an atmosphere of evangelism within the Church. Every endeavor they have undertaken, or undertaking or will undertake in the interests of the Church, will have little value in God's sight if they are not ultimately geared towards the expansion of the kingdom and the advancement of the soul-winning effort. Yes, it is very commendable, indeed absolutely necessary, to amass the financial, material and structural instrumentalities for the church. But all such effort must be primed towards the pursuit of evangelism. For what endeavor will take precedence over, or supplant the pre-eminence of the Great Commission and impress God more?

Hear God: "Where is the house that you will build Me........Where is the place of My rest? For all these things My hand has made...........but on this will I look: on him who is of a broken and contrite spirit and trembles at my word" (Isaiah 66:2). We can't impress God with what His very own Hands have made. The psalmist concurs: "The earth is the Lord's and its fullness thereof" Everything on the earth already belongs to God. He is impressed with no less than broken and contrite hearts trembling at His laws and trembling at His Command to go out and preach the gospel, winning more broken and contrite hearts that will tremble at God's word!

It is amazing how the grand manipulative scheme of the enemy is playing out right before our very eyes, we see it and yet we still don't 'see' it. For those who do not know, the harsh reality is that our focus is being manipulated away from our fundamental and most critical assignment: soul-winning. Indeed the principalities and powers of wickedness in high places have their strongest weapon in manipulation- manipulating us into complacency, procrastination, intimidation and distraction. Alas we

know just as much as the enemy knows that he can't stop our eternal liberation, but he can lull us into dragging our feet. This is all in a bid to paralyze us and make us neglect exactly that which will quicken our eternal liberation. Christ's Second Coming will not be hastened by the Church's shoddy stewardship to the Great Commission. It is very possible that God may be restraining the second coming of His son to give the teeming masses of lost souls a chance to 'enter the ark' before the great and terrible day of the Lord. The scriptures tell us that God does not desire that any perish but that all have everlasting life. There are lots of lost souls that God desires to save before the eternal curtain falls. How are they going to be saved if we do not reach and aggressively evangelize them? Secondly, let no one be left in any doubt: Christ will not hasten His return for the Church until it is unified and of one accord. He is not coming back for a discordant and disordered Body. The scriptures tell us that on the day of Pentecost, "they were all in one accord".
As a matter of fact, the verse reads: "......when the day of Pentecost was fully come, they were all with one accord......." (Acts 2:1).

The second verse tells us what happened next: "and suddenly, there came a sound from heaven.....".
Note the words 'fully' and 'suddenly'. What these words emphasize is that the fullness of a conducive atmosphere for the arrival of the Holy Spirit occurred when they were all with one accord....and immediately, the Holy Spirit showed up.

They had to be on one accord before the Holy Spirit would descend. Just as the Holy Spirit descended only when the atmosphere of one accord was in place, so can we expect Christ to descend for the Church only when a similar atmosphere prevails among the brethren. This bespeaks unity. EVEN THOUGH WE ARE IN PARTS IN SO MUCH AS DENOMINATIONS ARE CONCERNED, WE MUST NOT FORGET THAT WE ARE STILL PARTS OF ONE BODY AND WE MUST NOT underestimate the importance of unity in the Body. The God we serve Himself is unity personified, exemplified and amplified. His fullness is amplified in the unified Father, Son and Holy Ghost.

Let us briefly probe the essence of parts. God Himself epitomizes the mystery, beauty, simplicity and complexity of parts. He is diversity Personified, three Parts in One and One in three Parts, all functioning in perfect love and harmony. His creation itself is diversity exemplified and amplified- the diverse cosmic elements and nature all functioning in harmony and stabilized by harmony. God in three distinct and functional Parts is the ultimate exemplification of love and harmony in action: harmony of purpose and harmony of action; harmony in Parts and harmony of Parts.

Without love between the Parts there can be no harmony of the Parts. Love enables the harmony of the Parts and the very Parts in themselves precipitate the evolution and manifestation of love which in turn perpetuates the harmony. Since God is love, and all His laws are summarized in love, it is inevitable that the manifestation of love and those things that evoke love will be His pre-occupation.

Is it any surprise that the existence of parts within the Body of Christ offers the perfect backdrop for the interplay and outplay of love at its purest?

Brethren, this is food for thought. Where is love among us? Where is harmony among us? Where is unity among us?

The Church must appreciate the fact that disunity hamstrings its potential. Disunity and discord are unlike God and this is why He cannot be a partaker in such. This is why disunity within a disunited Church retards the operation of the Holy Spirit. This is why disunity within and between congregations has got to disappear. The discord has got to go in order that the Church may unleash the fullness of the power of the Holy Spirit to evangelize powerfully.

LOOK AT WHAT HAPPENED AFTER THE HOLY SPIRIT WAS UNLEASHED POWERFULLY ON THE DAY OF PENTECOST. OVER 3000 SOULS WERE SAVED IN ONE DAY! THIS IS THE KIND OF EXPONENTIAL SOUL-WINNING PROWESS WE CAN EXPECT TO FLOW FROM THE HOLY SPIRIT THROUGH US IF ONLY WE WILL EMULATE THE EXAMPLE OF THE FIRST CHRISTIANS. IF ONLY WE WILL READ THE HANDWRITING ON THE WALL! IMAGINE SUCH AWESOME ANOINTING TURNING LOOSE AMONG US IN THESE LAST DAYS! IF ONLY WE WILL UNIFY AND BE OF ONE ACCORD AS THEY DID BACK THEN! IF ONLY..... MAY GOD HELP US!

We must not allow complacency to paralyze us. God demands that we intensify, multiply and build on the Church outreach effort thus far. But how can we hope to do this effectively if we do not eradicate the disunity that retards the full outpouring of the power of the Holy Spirit? If the Church does not unite, how can it confront a united foe? The kind of unity being talked about here is not necessarily a physical assemblage of all denominations under one roof.. The Church does not need to merge physically before it can be united. The unity being talked about here is oneness of accord, a unity of purpose and a unity of direction among all Christ-centered denominations. If God is not calling for an obliteration of denominations at this time, He is demanding unity in our denominational diversity and a harmonization of the Church soul-winning objective. Evangelism must be intensified. It must be elevated to the highest priority.

We need to start with the lost souls in our immediate neighborhoods. We see them in the locale of our churches, around and about on our way to and from worship-the homeless, the hungry, the alcoholic, the drug addicted, the mentally disturbed, the sex traders-images of the walking dead.

These are the very ones that God has specifically sent an explicit message that we should go to. Nashville, take up the mantle of aggressive and systematic co-operative evangelism and lay an example for the world. Why not? Pastors can be key movers here. Brethren should be exhorted to make evangelizing an everyday thing, at work, at home, in the public places, in the neighborhoods.
Churches should organize evangelism-training programs for all members. Pastors should relentlessly hammer the evangelism imperative from behind the pulpit. It has become priority number one in these last days. The last days are surely here and God is about to move mightily into harvest mode. The Church must move when God says move. The Church must move in sync with God. Churches must move out into their neighborhoods and witness to the lost.

Area congregations especially neighborhood churches, can be divided into joint action zones where churches in the same area/locality can come together into units and sub-units for co-operative evangelism, outreach events etc. The entire gamut of evangelical/outreach activities ought to be an ongoing effort.

Well-organized evangelism ministries can be set up to act as key organs of coordination for each congregation's outreach effort. The ministries may be constituted of specialized teams charged with specific duties i.e., witnessing teams, prayer teams, follow-up teams, counseling teams, care and comfort teams, transport teams etc.

The above are basic pointers in the direction we need to go. Satan, our foe is well organized and we need to organize and consolidate before we can confront and conquer him. I imagine it will be very easy for the undiscerning to dismiss this as the figment of an overzealous imagination. Let whosoever be reminded that this is not about me but about God and His purpose; that it is by His grace that the lowly are chosen for His glory and that the lowly are precious in His kingdom. Praise His Mighty Name! By His grace, Nashville now gets to see the big picture-God is in the final Harvest mode and He wants to unify His Church. These two processes are precipitators of the Second Coming of Christ.

What God wants to start in Nashville could mushroom all across America and the entire world if we are obedient and fervently responsive to God. As this message goes out, God wants us to bear this in mind-it is up to us to make something or nothing of this call. What we make of it will determine how much it rocks the world. God is ready if we are.

Christians of all races and denominations would do well to lay aside the DEADWEIGHTS of denominational

SEPARATISM and racial prejudice, realizing that the redeeming Blood that flows through us is the same. It is the same Blood for the Black, White, or Yellow Christian. It is the same Blood for brethren at COGIC, Methodist, Baptist, Church of Christ.....whatever. It is the same Blood for whosoever will. Hallelujah to the Lamb!

We should count ourselves blessed in Nashville that God wants to use us to be the watershed of what could be part of a monumental revolution to pave the way for the return of his Son Jesus to this sick world.

So let us all, with humility, fervency and gratitude join hands, hearts, efforts and resources with the Holy Spirit to further this noble objective.

To Him who says "Surely I am coming quickly" be all the power, glory and hallelujah for ever more. Amen. Even so, come Lord Jesus!

Minister Sam Koya is currently the co-facilitator of the College ministry at Mt. Zion Baptist church. Prior to this, he had served as the assistant coordinator of the CARE ministry and had also served as a youth minister at the Grace United Methodist Church in Memphis, TN. He joined the Mt. Zion congregation in October 1997 and has since served in several ministries including the evangelism, prayer and prison ministries. The founder of Soul2Soul ministries (a college campus-focused ministry), Minister Sam Koya has a rich international cultural and educational background. He has lived and studied in Europe and Africa, his academic achievements include a Bachelor's Degree in Political Science, a Masters Degree in Business Administration and a Graduate Diploma in Comparative Politics. He speaks fluent Norwegian and some Swedish..

MINISTER ERWIN G. LEE

"IT'S AT THE WELL"

(JOHN 4: 7-13)

As people of God, we are always willing to go that extra mile to help those who are hurting and suffering. Anytime we see some one hurting or down, we want to talk to them or give them words of encouragement, you know try to meet there needs. However, there is always a time in which we just feel tired. You know, those times we always do for the church and the church doesn't do for you when you are on your back; when you help everyone else with their problems but nobody wants to hear about yours; or when a rough financial season hits someone's life, it seems like you are the ATM machine, but when you need money others have the "out of order" sign up. This is a time when you get sick and tired of anyone and everything and your cup, which is charity, is empty. Anybody feel like that today? Well the Lord wants to tell you to hold on and take a sip of the Living Water.

Now I know you may want to throw in the towel and may not feel like giving anymore. You may ask the question, "How can I refill my cup so I can serve God?" If we go through John 4: 7-13, we will find three ways to deal with an empty cup.

The first way to deal with this dilemma is to know whom to please. In verses 7-9, we see Jesus ask a Samaritan woman for a drink of water. Her response was that she was a Samaritan and He was a Jew. The woman, in this case suffered from two states: the state of fear and lack of knowledge. Fear because of her sex and status in the community and lack of knowledge because she did not know who asked to serve her. If we are to fill our empty cups we must know why we are doing certain things. We must think why are we helping or why are we giving and giving and no one gives to us. We are trying to bless others so that God may be glorified. When that person comes for that word of encouragement, remember you are representing the King. Don't worry if no one helps you when you are down because the Prince of Peace is there to help dry every tear from your eye and counsel in your weakest moment.

The second way we know how to keep our cups filled is to realize where our strength comes from. In verses 10-12, we see Jesus telling the woman if you serve me with what I asked, I, as the Son of God, will supply you with Living water or eternal life. The woman, in verses 11 and 12 still thinks Jesus is still speaking of the water in the well. She then begins to receive revelation of who this may be.

Unfortunately, this is how we can be. There are times when the Lord may be doing a work in our lives and we don't even know it. I remember always asking God, "What ministry do you have for me?" Even though every job I had was with and everywhere I went, children were drawn to me, I still asked God, "So, what do you want me to do?" You see, when your cup runs empty, we to realize that even tough we are drained, even though we seem unappreciated, we have to that God is our strength and comforter and He is always with us. No matter how tired we get, we need to tap into the power that God has for us. Finally, when our cup is empty, we have to learn to take a drink of the living water. In verse 13, Jesus says that if you drink this water in the well, the lady would still thirst. However, if she drinks of the living water that only Jesus could give, she would have eternal life. Jesus is using certain words here as symbols. Water is used throughout the Bible to represent life. In other words, Jesus wants the woman, which represents us, to drink the life that can help us to keep on going.

When you are at a place where you feel used up or mistreated, go to the well. At the well, take a drink of the one who is life. When you feel like what you are doing is in vain, go to the well. When you are doing most of the work while everyone else is being trifling, go to the well. When people laugh at you because you are serving God, go to the well. At the well, we will receive His power. At the well, we will receive His grace. At the well, we will receive His love. At the well, we receive his peace that passes all understanding.

There was a time when my cup ran empty. I thought I had to please everyone all the time. I had to be in every ministry and club that I could join. Yeah, I had to be every man to everybody. It took me losing my education at Vanderbilt University to realize that I was doing too much. Even though I felt used up, tired and distraught, I learned that I could not please God by being in every ministry or doing too much. I've learned that when every thing is crumbling down and when no one is around to help, to go to the well and take a sip of the living water. Is there someone today who feels like they are on empty? I invite you to go to the well with me and take a sip of the Living water.

Minister Erwin G. Lee was born on June 28, 1973 in the Bronx, New York. After graduating from Mt. St. Michael Academy in 1991, Minister Lee attended Fisk University in Nashville, Tennessee, receiving his B.A. in Biology/Pre-

Med in 1995.

In the year 1996, God had another plan for Minister Lee. He received his call to the ministry and a license to preach at Mt. Zion Baptist Church in Nashville, Tennessee where Dr. Joseph Warren Walker is the senior pastor. Currently, Minister Lee attends Lipscomb University where he will be receiving a Master in Divinity degree in 2001. He also works in the youth ministry at Mt. Zion Baptist Church and is an Editor at the National Baptist Publishing Board/R.H. Boyd Publishing Corporation. He is happily married to Libby Flewellen Lee and they are expecting their first child in November 2000. Most importantly, he is willing to serve God and help others in any capacity needed.

Minister Ralph T. Lofton
Director of Music Ministries

"REACH FOR IT"

Writer/Ralph Lofton, CMI Inc.
Publisher/RaphTon Music, BMI

(Malachi 3.10, Mark 11.24)

Ist Verse:

Lead: If you need Joy, Reach!
Background: Reach for it!
Lead: If you need the Holy Ghost, Reach!
Background: Reach for it!
Lead: Anything you need, its there within your reach, if you know
the God I know, you will receive.
Background: Yeah!

2nd Verse:

Lead: If you want a blessing, Reach!
Background: Reach for it!
Lead: if you need a healing, Reach!
Background: Reach for it!
Lead: There is nothing hard, nothing that my GOD can't solve, He'll
open up the windows, and send you down a blessing.
Background bridge: When you need Him most, He is there for you.
Lead: You can trust Him in everything you do.
Background: You must believe in Him, to receive from Him.

Lead: All the love He has He'll give it to you.
Background: All we have to do is just live right.

Vamp

Background: Yeah (repeat 2nd verse through background bridge)
Yeah (Repeat 2nd verse through the background bridge)
You better believe! Reach for it (repeat), if you need a blessing. Reach for it,
Writer/Ralph Lofton, CMI Inc.
Publisher/RaphTon Music, BMI

"So Glad I'm Saved"

Writer/Ralph Lofton, CMI, Inc.
Publisher/RaphTon Music, BMI
May 11, 1991

Chorus: So glad I'm saved, so glad I'm saved.
So glad I'm saved, so glad I'm saved.

1st Verse: I've got to live my life like he wants me to,
I've got to spread the word, that's what he wants me to do.
I won't let nobody, turn me around.
I'm gonna stay the course, and stand my ground.

God is coming back, to take us to his place,
You want to be in this Christian race.
The only way is by his power divine.
Through new life, Sublime!

Chorus: So glad I'm saved, so glad I'm saved,
So glad I'm saved, so glad I'm saved.

2nd Verse: Jesus paid the price, for all of our lives,
He gave his life, so we could be free,
I'm glad his spirit, lives in me.
You've got reservations, to be with him,
The only thing he want, is you to be free,
From sin.
I'm leaning on his everlasting arms.
He keeps me safe, from all harm.

Bridge: (Lead) He can save your soul, (Background)
If you let him in.
No matter what you've done, he will free
you from sin.
He's knocking at the door, the door of your
heart.
(Background) He can save, he can save,
your soul!

"Rejoice He's Coming"
Writer/Ralph Lofton, CMI, Inc.
Publisher/RaphTon Music, BMI

Chorus Rejoice he's coming, rejoice he's coming,
rejoice he's coming,
rejoice he's coming back to take us home.

(Repeat)

Verse 1 You may think that it's all a lie when he said
he's coming to take us high.
I want you to know, you better be ready.
He's prepared a glorious place, on his word
he promised there would be

enough space.
No need to worry, no need to fear, God is coming back to get us to the hills, Rejoice!

Chorus

Rejoice he's coming, rejoice he's coming, rejoice he's coming,
rejoice he's coming back to take us home.

(Repeat)

Verse 2

There are times when you feel distressed, every thing you seem to
try makes you feel more depressed.
There's only one thing, to relieve the presure sure.
Just a word from the Lord will do, on his word he promised to carry us through.

No need to, (Fret, he hasn't failed us yet).

Background

God is coming back to, (get us and take us to the sky) Background

Rejoice, yeah. Seek ye the Lord while ye may be found. Call ye upon him, while he is near.

There's no need to, (Fret, he hasn't failed us yet). Background
God is coming back to, (get us and take us to the sky).

Vamp

(Background) Rejoice he's coming back again ----.
And we will never be the same ----Rejoice.

Repeat

Verse 3 There's no need to, (Fret, he hasn't failed us yet).

Vamp Rejoice he's coming back again ----
And we will never be the same ---- Rejoice.
And vamp out.

"Be Ready"

Writer/Ralph Lofton, CMI, Inc.
Publisher/RaphTon Music, BMI
May 7, 1991

Verse 1 You better be ready, cause he's coming back again,
Don't let him catch you, caught up in your sins.
Clean up your house, so you can receive him when he comes,
Don't let him show up, and your works undone.

Chorus You better be ready, you don't know the hour.
You better be ready, cause he's coming back with Power.
You better be ready, when that Great trumpet sound.
You better be ready when he comes.

Verse 2 Jesus said be ready, for you don't know the day,
He's coming back, I pray you don't hesitate.
If you're prepared, the thief will pass you by,
Be in that number, so you can meet him in the sky.

Chorus You better be ready, You don't know the hour,
You better be ready, cause he's coming back with Power.
You better be ready, when that great trumpet sound,
You better be ready, when he comes.

Bridge

Lead When the Son of man comes.

Background The angels will be with him.

Lead All nations will gather before him.
We'll be separated, some on the left, some on the right.
If you're on the right, then you will have, Eternal life.

Repeat Chorus and Bridge

Vamp Be ready, (Background)
He is coming. (Lead)
Be ready, (Background)
Don't hesitate. (Lead)
Be ready, (Background)
Clean up your house (Lead)
Be ready (Background)
Before its too late (Lead)
Be ready when he comes. (Background)

Vamp Repeat until out.

At the age of nine, Ralph's career began while attending Sunday school. Sadie C. Ambrose, his God sent motivator, asked him to play the closing song on the piano. At first he was reluctant, after all he had never played before. He stepped forward, sat at the piano and thought, "What am I going to do?" Mrs. Ambrose asked the audience to sing and for Ralph to catch on as they sang, "Jesus Keep Me Near the Cross". As he lifted his hands, God anointed him with the ability to play the cords to the song. As he played, the Lord came into the Sunday school room and the Spirit began to move, the more he played, the higher the spirit rose. From that miraculous blessing and the endearing support of his mother, Mrs. Sarah Lofton, he took music lessons.

In 1984, the Lord moved Ralph from his home in Memphis to Nashville, Tennessee where he played the organ and the piano for several churches, until 1986. He was then introduced to Bobby Jones and New Life. After hearing Ralph play, Bobby Jones hired him as a keyboard player for his internationally known television show, Bobby Jones Gospel, seen on Black Entertainment Television (BET). This group recorded on of Ralph's first songs. Ralph remained affiliated with this organization until February 1994.

Ralph is the owner and President of RaphTon Music and Publishing Company. He attained recognition as a BMI songwriter and publisher. He is affiliated with various music companies such as Warner Brother, Warner Alliance, Word Records, Epic, Sony, Benson Company, Malaco, Savoy, Blackberry, EMI Gospel and Jo-Niece Records, just to name a few.

Ralph has performed with such artists as: The Nashville

Symphony, The San Francisco Symphony, Patti Austin, Whitney Houston, Clifton Davis, Steve Wonder, Take 6, BeBe and CeCe Winans, The Williams Brothers, Beverly Crawford and Shirley Ceasar. Ralph has appeared in many television productions such as: The Arsenio Hall Show, Regis and Kathy Lee, The Today Show and the Trinity Broadcast Network and various video performances.

Ralph has a loving, supportive and inspirational wife, Cleotra and has four sons: Bret, Deon, Radhun and Thomas.

"Trust in the Lord, and do good;...Delight thyself in the Lord; and He shall give thee the desires of thine heart."
(Psalms 37:3-4)

Minister Charles E. McCutcheon

"What Happens When Men Pray"

(Matthew 6: 5-15)

When I was a boy, I was taught several things that were incorrect about prayer. I was taught to recite the Lord's Prayer. Although I was taught that prayer would get me things, I hardly ever got the thing in which I prayed. I was told I was talking to God, which in other words there was a one way conversation being held in which God did not participate. Lastly, I was told as a boy that Good people pray while Bad ones did not. This means that I only prayed because I didn't want to be a Bad person, not to get a relationship, in other words, it was all about me.

One has to know to whom they are praying. One has to develop or have a relationship with God to pray to God, recognizing who he is to you as Christian. When we become grown men and live a little with sin trouble, reality forces us to abandon our childhood belief that God hears our prayers. Maybe we were never taught pray as a child or no one taught us, if we pray to this invincible spirit, mystically and magically bring it to pass. Some of us are willing to believe in prayer until we try it and it doesn't work. Then we're back where we started believing in nothing and wondering why it works for some people and not for us. Could it be we don't understand the purpose of prayer and the mechanics (spiritual Laws of Prayer)? Let's examine a prayer that is commonly known as the Lord's Prayer, which is Matthew 6: 5-15. Verses 5-8, Jesus explains the purpose and attitude on e should have when they pray. If one knows a lot of things, they should not use it to

impress people or God with your ability to string together catch phases or beautiful words. Men may be impressed, but God knows mans' attention will be all you receive for your efforts. Do in private and from your heart. Remember that God always know what you need when you hurt and what you have done. You don't have to hide anything or be ashamed. If you do pray in secret, God will reward you openly, recognize your closure and help you handle any situation you come across. Verse 8 shows it's not a prayer at all, but a blue print of how to pray.
"Our father"- relationship. God knows you and you know him. He knows you because you spend time in prayer talking to God telling him what really is on your mind. The things you wouldn't admit to anyone, sometimes not even yourself!

"Hollowed" - holy, respectful one to be respected and honored, because of who he is!

"Thy Kingdom Come" - His right to rule over us.

"Thy will be done" - his way of doing things on earth as it is in heaven.

"Give us this day our daily bread" - Jesus is the word, the word is bread. We need his word everyday to live a victorious life. His word is the only weapon to fight the devil.
"Lead us not into temptation" - Help us not to do things that world destroy us or belittle us or rob us of our family or our church family (forgiveness has to be given before it can be received). Help us make the right choices that lead to a Godly life. In John 10:10, Jesus said that I come that you might have life and have it more abundantly.

"Thine is the kingdom" it is his house, he makes the rules. He is the power in control not us. The glory forever and ever. You can count on him he'll never change. He will always be large and in charge and he is there for (insert your name here).

Thank you Jesus!

All glory be to God!

Minister Charles McCutcheon

Charles McCutcheon was born to Childress and Mary McCutcheon. Charles served as an Associate Minister and Youth Pastor at Jackson Street Baptist Church from 1995 to 1997. Charles joined Mt. Zion Baptist Church-Nashville in the spring of 1997 and currently serves on the Ministerial Alliance and is one of the founding members of the Children's Church.

To a friend & Brother
I pray that God bless you
always
Charles S. McCutcheon

Minister Price M. McKinney

"Suffering For The Cause Of Christ"

(1Peter 4:12-19)

Many people undergo situations and circumstances in life and never come to understand why they go through what they're going through. Therefore we have a negative response and unpleasant reactions towards whatever transpires. We get mad, we fly off the handle. We cuss, fight and groan and the predicament still doesn't go away. You must come to realize that things will happen to make you suffer. And when you don't know what or who you're suffering for, it becomes uncomfortable, misunderstood and it seems foreign and unfair. We pray and our prayer goes unanswered, so then we ask, "Lord, why me?" We look for outlets of rescue - still not change. I would like to with God's help, help you with your suffering.

1) As Partakers of Christ's Sufferings. It is Purposely Planned For Your Purification. In verses 12 and 13, Peter opens up by saying "Beloved"- talking to Christians. Don't be alarmed. God loves you too much, He wants the best out of us. So, he takes us through the fiery trials. "That the trial of your faith, being much more precious than of Gold that perisheth. Though it be tried with fire, might be found unto praise and honour and glory at the appealing of Jesus Christ." (1Peter 1:7) Gold, when it is purified, has to be burned by fire in order for the impurities to be released. God takes us through the fire to get us to purity. But Rejoice! Be glad and over and above glad, that you actively participate in Christ's sufferings. Great is your reward to come.

2) When You Suffer, Know Whether It's For Your Position or Your Disposition. In verses 14-16, Here sufferers are distinguished by when what you do becomes who you are. If you suffer for Christ, happy is what you should be. But, to suffer for Christ is to understand why Christ suffered! Why, what and who did he suffer for? So that God may be glorified! "yea, and all that live godly in Christ Jesus shall suffer persecution." (2Timothy 3:12) This is your position and because of it, the Holy Spirit lives within you and God is glorified due to your allowance to suffer for him. "Let your light so shine before men." (Matthew 5:16) "Blessed are ye, when men shall deceive you and persecute you and say all manner of evil against you falsely for my sake." (Matthew 5:11)

Verse 15 points out that, now we've got those who suffer for disposition. Disposition being the way you think, react and behave. These are those who suffer for doing evil. This form of suffering is carnal. It brings misery, injustice, hurt, harm and danger to themselves as well as those around them. But, those who suffer for Christ, because they bear the name Christian, be strong, be proud and stand firm!

3) Suffering For Christ Brings Commitment To The Creator. Our Judgement is coming soon and it will start with us - "The House of God". In order for it to be a house of God, He must be there. For God to be there, you must let him in. If we who are saved barely become saved, how awful will the doom be which his mercy saves us? (Jeremiah 25:29). When you suffer for Christ, it lines up with the Word of God and the will of God. Committing your soul to him means you must be obedient in well doing (Galatians 6:9 and 1Peter 3:19). Committing your soul means that you trust him as Lord! Suffering For The Cause

Of Christ is just a part of God's purification process. Amen.

"Go On"

Things are OK, not too bad,
Right now I can hang.
Suddenly you're delivered the news,
It's a devastating bang.
It happened so quick. There's no way
To prepare.
Your mouth falls to the floor.
You say, "Boy I Swear!"
"What's next? How much more?"
Are the questions we ask.
Struggle after struggle, Pain after pain
Why is life such a task?
You try to do right with everything
In your power.
Misery, suffering, heartache, mess
Always seem to shower.
You're pushed to the point where you
Scream "That's Enough!"
As soon as you get over this,
Here's comes more stuff.
You're fed up, frustrated, soon
Ready to retire.
Questioning, wondering, "Does this
Pain ever expire?"
Where are you now? Where were you then?
Just take a glance.
Somehow, someway you survived
Chance after chance.
Each time you feel, you got back
Up again
Even if you were all along, without
The help of a friend.
No matter what the situation, you

Did overcome.
But that's that game of life,
You win some- you lose some.

Don't stop. Continue to press.
Please, don't quit.
Square your shoulders. Take one step.
Yes! You can make it.
I know you're hurt. I feel your pain.
You ask, "How long?"
Pray and cry, feed your faith, but
My friend, Do Go On!!

"Weary At Work"

We all get frustrated, angry, mad as hell.
So much built up inside. Not a soul we can tell.
We carry the load, the weight of people and much more,
Hours later clock out. Your body and mind completely sore.

We drive home "swoll-up", scarred from today's mess.
Mind clouded, feelings hurt, don't want to hear "God Bless".
The emotions rise, keep going up, only to bring pain.
Often times makes you sit and wonder "Is this considered gain?"

Sometimes life seems unfair. The good people never win.
Each day a new sunrise so we can start again.
The good thing about today is tomorrow it's in the past.
Therefore, what you feel is just for a moment. Forever it will not last.
So right now I say to you my friend, tray to let it go.
But if you don't I do understand. But one thing you must know.
In the midst of the dark shines a star big and bright.

It's radiant, easy to see and brings forth much light.
It beams down from the sky way up above.
Made high in the heavens only a token of God's love.
When the rain pours down, does its work. Its damage it leaves behind

There's something else to remember and always keep in mind.
Soon may come the colored arch that we call a rainbow
To face it brings a smile, a quite stunning glow.
I'm simply passing on what's been given so freely to me.
Fun, joy, friendship, jokes and how to live happily!
I know you're tired, ready to quit and that's putting it politely.
But deep down there's a light within that will continue to shine so brightly!!

Minister Price M. McKinney

Price McKinney is a native of Knoxville, Tennessee and is an integral part of Mt. Zion's Ministerial Alliance. Price currently serves as the primary instructor/facilitator for the Men's Sunday Bible Institute Class and along with his wife Sharon, assist in the church's "Covenant Marriage" class. He and Sharon have two sons, Chris and Price Jr.

God Bless You!!
Price M. McK '00

Elder Allyataye Russ

"Amazing Grace"

Ephesians 2:8-9

For by grace are ye saved through faith; and that not of yourself: it is the gift of God: Not of works lest any man should boast.

"Amazing grace how sweet the sound that saved a wretch like me, I once was lost but now I'm found, was blind but now I see," are the words of a song that has touched lives and hearts for generations. This hymn has caused many to recognize the love of God like never before. It rings in our ears like the words in the National Anthem, the Star Spangled Banner, 23rd Psalms and the Lords prayer. It's almost breath taking when one considers God's great kindness that has been extended to us. However, my concern is whether or not we understand this thing called grace. Grace is God's unmerited or undeserved favor. The word of God said that Jesus died on the cross for our sins. That's Grace! The word says that his blood could make us whole again. That's Grace!

Why do we say it's amazing? One of the things that makes grace so amazing is the fact that it's free. I believe that one of the reasons why some don't accept this grace is because they are blinded by this world. The world teaches us that nothing in life is free. The philosophy of grace says that the best things in life are free. Please remember the acronym for Grace, God's Riches At Christ's Expense. Another thing that makes grace so amazing, is the fact that not everyone will receive it. That's why I believe Paul was able to write the words that are written in these verses of Ephesians because he understood grace. Paul, formerly known as Saul, was a murderer, he was disobedient to the things of God and lost in a world of sin but one day as he was on his way to Damascus he heard the voice of Jesus and it radically changed his life forever, it was the voice of grace sent to save his sinful soul. That day Paul discovered the depth of God's love and the riches of his amazing grace.

A couple of years ago, the newspaper carried a story about a man that was a seasoned paratrooper with over 800 jumps to his credit. He was also a skilled photographer. He spent his time recording the jumps of skydiving teams with his video equipment. On one such occasion, he prepared his equipment and jumped with the divers. With great skill he followed the divers with his camera focused continuously on them, recording their every move. The skydivers completed their maneuvers and opened their parachutes. It was time for him to do the same. He reached for his ripcord, it was then that he discovered, to his horror, he had forgotten to put on his parachute. Imagine the panic that gripped him as he realized his imminent death, a death that could have so easily been avoided.., If only he had made proper preparations. So it is with grace. Grace is amazing, isn't it? What will people do on that great day of judgement without Grace (their parachute)? Therefore, be sure my friend to ask the Lord for your daily grace before you jump into your daily life!

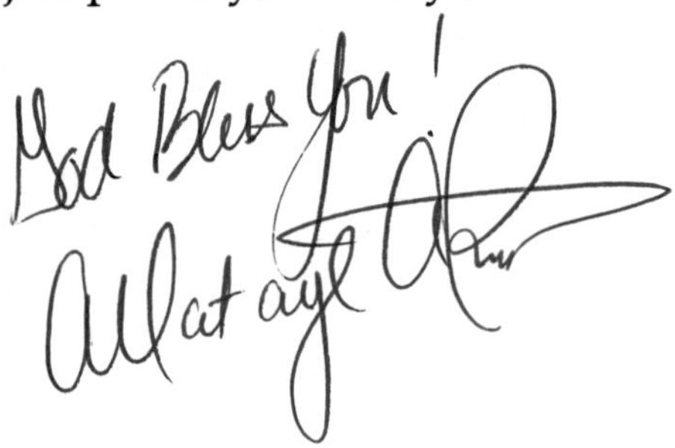

Elder Allataye Russ

"Cast your Cares!"

1 Peter 5:7

Casting all your care upon him; for he careth for you.

Do you realize that everything that concerns you concerns our God. God constantly and consistently oversees your well being. There's nothing too big or too small in our lives over which God has no concern. God cares so for us that even the strands of hair on our heads are numbered. I must admit that I have a habit of saying TAKE CARE and AND BE BLESSED. However, God never instructed us to take care; God wrote through the Apostle Peter commanding us to CAST OUR CARES. When you cast your care it gives God control over your situation but when you take care, it leaves you in control. As a professional fisherman the Apostle Peter wrote so eloquently about casting ones cares. For scripture says, "Cast our cares upon him; for he careth for you." You've got to be purposeful with your casting, you can't cast you cares around or upon everyone. The scriptures teach us not to cast our pearls, that which is precious, among the swine. Notice, he did not say cast your cares upon your friend, boss, family or even oneself, because not everyone that's around you has your best interest at heart. The scriptures says to cast your cares upon Him (Jesus) for he cares for you. Do your problems and situations seem to hard to bear? Cast your care! Do your bill collectors give you a scare? Cast your care! Does sin try to put you in its snare? Cast your care! Does your situation with your family or friends give you a nightmare? Cast your care! When problems of life seem too hard to bare, give it over to Jesus in prayer end watch His miracles appear.

Elder Allataye Russ

"A Date at the Plate!"

Matthew 4:4

But he answered and said, It is written, Man shall not live by bread alone, but by every word that proceedeth out of the mouth of God.

Do you eat to live or do you live to eat? Does food seem to call your name. Is the refrigerator secure in your presence. Are you one of those individuals that seemingly must constantly have food in your mouth? Well, I have a message for you. Do you realize that over the last couple of years America, as a nation has become larger in size. Some of the studies completed by professionals indicate that, pound for pound, America has added tremendously to its collective growth. By in large, this is a result of the way our society functions. It appears that much of our leisure time is centered around ingesting massive quantities of foodstuffs, especially those delicacies commonly referred to as "junk food." From company meetings to casual conversation, from funerals to weddings, food is always at the core of our activities.

Another reason that America is getting larger results from our collective daily intake of substances placed in food. For example, because steroids are being utilized in the meat industry, trace elements appear in our diet. Injection of such chemicals is utilized with the desired results of producing a bigger and fatter animal. In doing so they unconsciously made America a bigger and fatter nation. Jesus said that Man should not live by bread alone but by every word that proceedth out of the mouth of God. Are you familiar with a concept referred to as sublimation? It's the process of diverting or re-channeling a behavior into a more acceptable form. For example, if there is a child that seems overly aggressive toward other children, one would attempt to re-channel this behavior by involving this person in sports such as football or karate in an effort to place the child in an environment suitable for such aggressive activity. Gluttony is a sin and I would be the first to admit to passed transgressions concerning this deadly sin. In spite of my pass failures to control my appetite appropriately, there is forgiveness if I recognize my sin and ask with a contrite heart for the Lord's forgiveness.

On the other hand, how much good could this country accomplish if we invested as much time ingesting spiritual food (THE WORD) as we spend dining at such palatial locations as McDonalds, Burger King, etc.. isn't it interesting how we go days and even months without feasting on the word, but fail to go days or even hours without our Big Macs and Whoppers, when our spiritual man is just as important as our natural man. Did you not know that the absence of hunger is the beginning of death. Remember the old cliche "you are what you eat?" Can you imagine Popeye without his spinach, or Scooby Doo without his Scooby snacks or a true Christian without the Word. Jesus taught his disciples to pray, give us this day our Daily bread. Finally, take the time to sit at the Masters table and feast on the best serving of food you can ever eat, the Word. Let the greatest Lover wine and dine you everyday. Amen!

Minister Adrian L. Scott, II

"ABSOLUTELY UNCONDITIONAL"

(John 13:33-38)

My children, yet a little while I am with you. Ye shall seek me: and as I said unto the Jews, Whither I go, ye cannot come; so now I say to you. A new commandment I give unto you, That ye love one another; as I have loved you, that ye also love one to another. By this shall all men know that ye are my disciples, if ye have love to one another. Simon Peter said unto him, Lord, whither I go, thou canst not follow me now; but thou shalt follow me afterwards. Peter said unto him, Lord, why cannot I follow thee now? I will lay down my life for thy sake. Jesus answered him, Wilt thou lay down thy life for my sake? Verily, verily, I say unto thee, The cock shall not crow, till thou hast denied me three times.

Peter was one of the disciples who loved Jesus and followed him throughout his journey. It was time for Jesus to leave his disciples for a little while, but before He left He wanted to give them something. Something so powerful it would separate the believer from the unbeliever, it would separate those who give lip service instead of life service. This would show all that you belong to Him. He gave them a new commandment: "Love one another as I haved loved you." This was not a new commandment, but to love others as much as Christ loved others is Revolutionary. Revolutionary means to turn a radical change. This kind of love would not only bring an unbeliever to Christ, but also give believers the strength and unity to handle a hostile world. This kind of love would break the devils hold on someone's child, crack the addiction of an addict, quench the thirst of a drunkard and even heal the blind, lame and the sick spiritually.

Jesus says to his disciples, " I will be with you only a little longer. You will look for me, and just as I told the Jews, so I tell you now: Where I am going, you cannot come." He says I will be in the midst of your situation a little while longer. I will reveal myself in your situation just for a little while longer, to help you understand, but I know you don't. I must go take care of some business that I told you about earlier.

Simon Peter, Simon for the old fisherman and Peter for the new person established in the relationship with Christ, "the Rock", asked him, " Lord (signifying he knows who Jesus is, relationship), where are you going?"
Jesus replied, " Where I am going, you cannot follow, but you will follow later."

Peter asked, " Lord, Why?". Have you ever asked God Why? Lord I've been a committed follower all these years, not a temporary follower like the crowds but I've given up my old life, my material possessions to be obedient to your word. Why are you going to leave me in this situation?
Peter says, " I will lay down my life for you. I will die for you, I will place my old self in a tomb and allow you to give my new life its purpose in which it was created for".

Then Jesus answered, "Will you really lay down your life for me? I tell you the truth, before the rooster crows, you will deny me three times! In Matt.26:69-75, Peter denies knowing Jesus. How many times have you denied Jesus as Lord of your life in one day everyday?

Jesus knows all about you and Peter, but yet He did not change the situation because the situation is designed to change you. Jesus knows exactly what you are going to do in your situations to hurt him, but yet He did not stop loving you unconditionally.

Peter wasn't honest with himself when he promised to stand by Jesus, no matter what the cost. He didn't realize he was following Jesus to the cross. When the situations got rough Peter backed out of his commitment.
Anything worth having cost something. Its easy to say we love Jesus when it doesn't cost anymore than just sitting in church on Wednesdays and Sundays, but the real test is being a living example for Christ as He was a living example for the Father.

It is better to be a follower who fails than one who fails to follow. Peter was a close follower who didn't understand. Do you understand! To love others as Christ loved others is love rooted in the mind and will of God and means to value, cherish, and devote to. This was taught by the Father giving His Son for man's salvation. This love is unconditional, experienced only through relationship.

Jesus said " A new commandment I give you: Love one another. As I have loved you, so you must love one another. By this all will know you are my disciples, if you love one another." All for the Sake of The Gospel.

Minister Scott is a new minister at Mt. Zion Baptist Church. He is married to wife, Konya M. Scott, three children, Kenneth, Markisha and Adrian, III. Employed with the Metro Nashville Fire Department as a firefighter II and emergency medical technician.

Minister Scott is presently a student at Belmont University, majoring in theology and minor in philosophy. He is a team member of Providence World Missions founded by grandfather, Pastor Willie L. Scott, an organization designed to save souls, build disciples, churches and schools in Uganda, East Africa.

Minister Scott desires to be a committed, obedient follower of Jesus Christ. He says, "it's better to be a follower who fails than one who fails to follow." Minister Scott's job is saving lives, but the saving of souls is his mission. All for the Sake of the Gospel!

"And Jesus came and spoke unto them saying, All power is given unto me in heaven and in earth. Go ye therefore, and teach all nations, baptizing them in the name of the Father, and of the Son, and of the Holy Ghost: Teaching them to observe all things whatsoever I have commanded you: and, lo, I am with you always, even unto the end of the world". Amen. Matthew 28:18-20.

MINISTER MELVIN V. WADE

"THE INTERTWINED AND THE INSPIRED"

(ACTS 3:1-8)

The book of ACTS written by Luke ,the physician, to Theophilus is a book of history and it can be summed up by the table of contents which are found in the first and second chapters. Content number one is the Christ. Luke wants it known that after the resurrection they saw Christ, they heard Christ, and they felt Christ.

The second content deals with the comforter, who is the Holy Spirit. Luke suggests that we need the comforter to enlighten us first to our memories secondly as to our movements lastly as to our message. Secondly, thing is we need the comforter to energize us to preach with power and to present the Christ like life. Thirdly we need the comforter to encourage us .The third content deals with the church which is seen praying, preaching, praising and prospering.

Now as we come to our text, Peter and John are together entering the temple for the three o clock prayer meeting. They stopped by a man, lame from his mothers womb seeking money. The text says he has been brought to this spot daily. This brings us to the first point of this story which is the intertwined. Peter and John are together by two things preaching and praying. These brothers, as it relates to preaching, were both called to ministry out on the seashore while fishing. Secondly, they were along with James. The captains of the other Apostles were apart of Jesus' inner circle not only were they together in preaching but praying also.

There are three things pointed out about prayer in this story. First, prayer is special. It is the Christian's family hour with our heavenly Father. Secondly, prayer is specific. The text says it was three o'clock which is one of the times the Jews had to pray. Next, the text gives the thing they were going to pray for which was to give thanks for the souls that were saved. Lastly, prayer is spectacular.

The text says that this man, which brings us to point number two, the interruption. He stops Peter and John on their way into the temple. This man has a serious defect condition. For this man is lame. He cannot walk. This condition is how sin left us after the fall of Adam.

We could not be free to move and be close to God. Of course that was before the events that occurred at the place of skull and before the grave, Sundays news of Christ's resurrection. Before we found out about this story, you and I were that lame man. But secondly, there are some lame Christians who have growth problems such as they do not study the scriptures, or ever witness, or/are stiff worshippers and they are spiritually less than two month old babies, still drinking milk with someone else holding the bottle. This man also has a sad dependence. It tells us he was poor because he asked for money, lute, cheese, cash which means he was a beggar. Scholars tell us he picked a good spot for a person who begged. For Jews went to pray at the temple three times a day; nine o clock, twelve o clock and three o clock. At the time of the text, the gate he chose was called Beautiful. It was so, because it was made of Corinthian bronze. This is said to have been during the prayer hours, when the area is full of people. This man figures that a praying person won't turn down a person in need. This man has a sole desire, he wants to walk.

The third point of the text is the interpretation. The scripture says that Peter and John asked the man to look on us with this statement the lame man's hopes are raised. With this man's hopes being raised Peter tells the man we don't have money but we have

Jesus. With this being stated Peter interpret the man's real problem his need for the master. Peter suggest a permanent solution not temporary one. The problem with Christianity is the lack of correct interpretation. We treat symptoms when in fact we should treat the root of the problem, sin. Secondly this man needs a miracle.

Finally, the inspiration the text says that Peter reaching forth with his right hand tells the man to rise up and walk. The man stands immediately his feet and ankle receive strength. The interesting thing about this is he skips the normal process of standing and walking. This man doesn't start by crawling first but he goes right to walking. Next, not only does this man stand he also shouts. The text says he enters the temple walking, leaping and praising God. When God performs a miracle like this you ought to shout too.

Minister Melvin Von Wade, Jr.

On October 11, 1969, Pastor and Mrs. Melvin Von Wade, Sr. gave birth to a bouncing baby boy in Dallas, Texas. Having lived in Dallas and Houston, Melvin, Jr. was educated in Los Angeles, California where he graduated from Westchester High School in 1988. Young Melvin continued his education at Santa Monica Junior College where he obtained a degree in Music. In August, 1999, Melvin, Jr. accepted his call to the ministry and in December, 1999 moved to Nashville, Tennessee to pursue a degree in Theology from American Baptist College. Melvin, Jr. is an active member of the Music Ministry at Mt. Zion Baptist Church.

BISHOP JOSEPH WARREN WALKER, III, D. MIN.

"THE OTHER BOY"

(LUKE 15)

Luke 15 records an episode in Divine script of a boy who left home to make it on his own. We know him as the prodigal son. He was a boy who was eager to get away.

The prodigal son left home pocket pregnant ready to give birth to a good time. Parents have often empathized with the father of this story. Certainly many parents have experienced the total disregard for appreciativeness that their children have engaged in. Nevertheless, our spirits are arrested when we tap into the emotions of the father as he reluctantly surrenders his son to a demonic society in order to teach him the real meaning of life.

We have heard the story told over and over of how this boy lived it up. He lived large and had friends in high places. His worldly gain though immoral and temporal was pleasing in the sight of a culture that embraced him. We are quickly reminded, however, that this boy who was on top of the world, had a collision with reality. Upon this collision, he found himself feeding pigs as a result of his wasted resources and ill-established friendships. It was at his

lowest ebb that he came to himself and was able to get a better view of his father's house, even from the pigpen.

This same boy who paraded through the streets living it and having a good time in the midst of a social high, found himself in a spiritual low. If he teaches us anything, he teaches us the degradation of lowliness. He teaches us of the dangers of buying into a culture that embraces "microwave" success. Success in an instant is the norm of the day. It is no secret that in our society today, many of our young people have chosen to travel the detours and shortcuts of life, rather than remain on the roads of toil and determination. But it is in this story that we see this boy coming to himself. He heads home, humble, repentant, and ready to start all over again. We are told of a father who saw him in a distance and ran to claim his son.

All of the hysteria---Daddy's best ring, best robe and the best calf are offered upon the boys return. All of this excitement over a son, who blatantly abused the privilege of being an heir. But the response of the father is not removed from many parents today. No matter how much trouble your children get in or how bad they are, you will hear this father's echo..."that's still my child." Love often defies rationale. It's in this story we see Jesus teaching us of a loving Father, whose grace and mercy stretches beyond reason. What good news! Regardless of his crime, his disposition with social and religious standards, IF and when he comes home, there's a great celebration on his being found. What a marvelous demonstration of grace!

Certainly we as a church should demonstrate this kind of love for our fallen brothers and embrace them with much celebration upon their return to the ranks of the Lord's army.

As the story proceeds, we are introduced to an elder brother whose anger and bitterness, at the celebration, did not represent the Kingdom of God. We as Christian's should shout the roof off when men put down their bottles and pick up their Bible. Yes there ought to be a celebration. Preachers have preached it over and over again. I have found myself engaging this text on numerous occasions. Here comes the son! But there is something about all of this. Though I like you am excited as well as ecstatic about the boys return, there is something many of us have tragically overlooked. While all of our resources were invested in the son who strayed away, and every eye focused on his every move, something was overlooked. While every finger was crossed and knee bowed in hopes that one day he would come to himself, we as a church have failed to celebrate the other boy who stayed home. Our resources are in a far country and our eyes our focused over yonder, while the boy in Sunday school who stayed home, never received his celebration. Just a pat on the back or a word of encouragement would do! There is another boy and the church though charged to find the lost son, must assure the boy who stayed home that he is most appreciated.

Yes even today, our newspapers are filled with the status of the prodigal son. One day he's holding up a store and the next he's selling drugs. The plight of the prodigal is ever before us. We pray and ask the Lord "When is he coming home?" Television monitors his plight. He's on COPS, sprawled on the head of a police care. He's Nino, a pimp and pusher in New Jack City, and he is Doughboy in Boyz in the Hood, a thief and hoodlum. He's on the evening news and the church, and every social institution that concerns itself with the future of African-Americans want to know when is he coming home. Most speeches and forums on the black male will consistently agitate your conscience by reminding you of the prodigal son's plight. Most sisters will tragically generalize all men, because they have experienced the wrath of the prodigal son. The church has been praying every Sunday that he would come off the corner, put down the bottle, get off the drugs, pull his pants up and come home. We've exhausted many of our resources
attempting to encourage the prodigal son to come home and at the same time we have not given recognition to the

other boy who stayed home. As a young pastor, I entered my ministry with a desire to reclaim our young black men. As a young man, the Lord has allowed me to identify with the plight of young people in 1993. Nevertheless, the other day as I was meditating, my spirit recalled a statement that I had briefly seen somewhere in my past. It was that statement that challenged my ministry to young people, more specifically to young black men. It simply says that: A man came to ministry with two basic choices. He stood of a mountain and observed young men leaning over a steep cliff. In his concern for their safety, he hurriedly ran over and asked them to stand away from the edge. As they willingly consented, he observed that down in the valley, were black men who had fallen off of the cliff. There were dope addicts, pimps, gang members and every other menace to society. He then heard a voice saying: "Either build a hospital in the valley, or Build a fence on the Cliff". That is the basic complication of the church of today. That statement challenges us to reconsider our focus and to channel our resources in different ways.

I must admit, that I have not decided whether I will build a cliff or a hospital, but I am certain that the church must face this challenge. The message of hope that we preach and teach is a message that builds hospitals in valleys. It goes way down in the valley and attempts to reconcile the outcast and those who have been counted out. But we must, as a people of faith, recognize the importance of building fences as well. What happens if we spend all of our time building hospitals in valleys? Those who stand on the cliff will fall as well. I am convinced that the church must sound the trumpet and the achievements of the other boy. If the church is serious about keeping the young men it has, it must make an effort to say that there are some good men in this world. There are so many adversaries to the young black male. This society that we live in perpetuates the glorifications of prodigal sons who have returned, and never gives due recognition to the boy who never left in the first place. Take for instance the gang member who puts down his gun. That's a wonderful testimony and the church should celebrate the reality of God's power to deliver. We should sound the trumpet, have it headlined in the newspaper and be excited about what the Lord has done. But I submit that if we go to that extreme for the gang member, we ought to go to that extreme for the child who resists the temptation of gangs and who received honors in school! If we fail to engage in this kind of recognition, our children will feel that the only way to be recognized by the church for accomplishments is by doing something horrendous and then "coming to themselves."

We as a church must nurture the kind of environment that embraces and encourages those children who stayed home. I thank God for the other boy. It's long overdue. Our world and our cities are filled with do-nothing, have-nothing and want to be nothing men. But at the same time there are men who have done something, who are doing something, and who are going to be something. We need to encourage them and honor them for their achievements. The other boys of our world have tragically been behind the scenes. There was a boy who got an "A" on his report card, but the newspaper thought the young black men who car-jacked made a better story. Here in Nashville, 3 young black men all under 17 were convicted of killing a clerk at a Hotel. The same night of the murder there was a young man teaching young people about the Bible. The news never caught his story. One of the reasons why the media does not recognize the achievements of our young black men is because we as a church and people have not demanded it. When we begin to recognize their accomplishments and focus more of resources toward building fences instead of hospitals, the media can't help but take us seriously. There are some implications here for the church. We have seen an exodus of a different kind as of lately. This exodus involves those that we nurtured through our Sunday Schools and Bible Studies. The church seems unable toretain it's children, and one of the reasons why is because other institutions rather religious or secular have embraced them. Our children are finding other arenas to express themselves, because the church consistently turns up her nose at the experiences of this generation. We must realize that this generation is so very different from any generation we've ever known.

Unless the walls of tradition are torn down or at least reconstructed, we will be unable to hold on to the boy we thought we had. That should be our concern. In most of our churches, the other boy experience a sort of silent pain, because his experiences are not validated and because gospel to him has meaning in a far country, but not at home. We can identify the prodigal son. It appears that his hostility and immorality make him more identifiable. But the other boy is less identifiable. He comes and suffers through the church's complacent posture on his expectations, and the insensitive generalizations that he has been placed in. The other boy is leaving our congregations in great numbers. We see him clean cut, standing on street corners uttering the truth as recorded by the Nation of Islam. His dedication and discipline are second to none. Why is he there and not in our churches, because instead of validating his experiences and recognizing and encouraging him, we were engaged in a debate about the state of the prodigal son? We must admit that we have failed to articulate our message to him. And because of this, he has migrated to where the message is articulated more clearly and has more meaning in his life. The other boy is leaving home as well.

It would be most unfortunate that we as a church continue to remain complacent in our posture of passivity. Certainly we can take issue with the other boy and blame him for his inconsistency and remind him that his accomplishments are recorded in glory. We can do that, but I am convinced that unless we as a church become more intentional about retaining the other boy, not only will we have a dilemma concerning the prodigal, but even the men we look at on Sunday and take for granted will "have fallen off the cliff." If the church is serious about the plight of the young black male and about fed up with lengthy debates concerning him, I suggest three principles that are necessary for retaining him. The very first is EMBRACING HIM. It is here that the words of the father in the parable come to mind. "You I have with me always..." This posture of security uttered by the father. The other boy in our congregation hears this utterance and assumes that he's taken for granted. No one embraces him.

No one celebrates the fact that he has remained faithful. Although his anger is wrong at the foundation, we must deal with the fact that many of our young black man justifiably hold this same anger. They hold it because the church has not embraced them. We must begin to embrace our young black men, more specifically the "other boys" in our churches. Embracing them implies, putting our arms around them and encouraging them to go on in spite of the odds. This means that we must exhaust ourselves in the perpetuation of positively and not wallow in negativity.

We must embrace the exile. The other boy is an exile. He has been exile by our inadvertantness. We must seek to embrace him in order that we might retain him. There are so many other institutions that are willing to embrace him, and the church must take the lead and demonstrate an unusual concern for the well being and welfare for the "other boy." Not only must we be concerned about embracing him, we must also concern ourselves with ENLIGHTING HIM. This implies that we must be able to articulate our faith and give it real meaning in the life of "the other boy". see in vs.31 and 32 that the father attempts to enlightening the other boy concerning what was going on? And we must seek to go beyond clichÈs and rhymes and really enlighten :the other boy". One of the reasons we have been unable to retain the celebration. Exegetically, I wondered did the boy get it?

Did he really understand prodigal is because we have not enlightened him, and it is certain that we are mandated to enlighten the other boy. We must enlighten him because he has been faithful. We must enlighten him as Paul enlightened Timothy. We must encourage him to be strong and endure hardness as a good solider. It does no good quoting statistics and reminded him of the number of men in college over against the number of men in prison. We must seek to focus on why and how those men got to college and encourage them to be all that they can be.

We must begin to dissect the word of God and articulate it in such a way that it has meaning in the life and experiences of the other boy. We can not assume that if he does not get the message that he did not listen. It is our responsibility to make sure that our message gets through and that he is able to carry that message to someone else. The faith of our fathers and mothers is what sustained us. Unless that faith is passed on to the other boy, he will not understand his religion outside of ecclesiastical expectations enlighten him. It is imperative that we ENGAGE HIM.

One of the assumptions and problems in many of our churches is that we have enough men who are visible. There are two here. One suggests that we are limited in our supply of men. The other suggests that we don't use the men we have. I tend to agree with both, but lean toward the latter. If we engage the men that we do have in our churches and stop complaining about the ones we don't have, maybe we will get other men who are on the outside. If we only seek to make the young black men in particular more visible in our congregations and engage them in the total work of the church, we might be able to reclaim more prodigals. One of the reasons our ministry in Nashville at the Mt. Zion Baptist church has been blessed with young black men is because we are very intentional about engaging them in the work of the church. I also might add that being a young Pastor also helps. But the majority of the men we have been able to evangelize say that to see young men up front engaged in the work for the Kingdom had a tremendous impact on their lives.

Our older generation must not become intimidated because the church engages young men. We must not get so wrapped up in positions and power that we miss the work of the Kingdom.

If we are serious about retaining the other boy, then we must engage him in the work of the church. We must move beyond the pacifism of reading a scripture on Men Day or teaching Sunday School on youth day. If we are serious, we must afford him the opportunity to head up ministries that address the needs of young black men. We must engage

him so that
he might engage us. I am thankful for the other boy. Although I may stand on a exegetical and hermeneutical island of pathos, I am glad that the other boy is succeeding in this drug invested society. He has proven that just because drugs are in the neighborhood, they don't have to be in his veins.

He has not consented to the argument that black folk don't make guns and uzzies as a justification for the violence perpetuated in his neighborhood.

He knows that blacks don't make them, but he also realizes that nobody forces him to buy and use them either. He has developed the spiritual capacity to rise above all the harsh things that are said of his gender. He has taught us that it's not what people call us that make us who we are, rather it's what we chose to answer to that matters. He has answered the call to manhood. He has demonstrated a sense of responsibility. Although we may not agree with his anger at the celebration, to know him is to understand it.

Bishop Joseph Warren Walker, III, D. Min.

Bishop Joseph Warren Walker, III was born in Shreveport, Louisiana on July 28th, 1967. He has received his B.A. from Southern University in Baton Rouge, Masters of Divinity from Vanderbilt Divinity School and his Doctorate of Ministry from Princeton Theological Seminary all with honors.

Bishop Joseph Warren Walker, III is the pastor of the Mt. Zion Baptist Church of Nashville, TN. He began his pastorate in the spring of 1992 with 175 members and presently the ministry has grown to over 6000 with over 1000 souls a year. Mt. Zion has 6 weekly services in 3 locations. He is the author of From Tragedy to Triumph and has a weekly television and daily radio ministry that blesses thousands across the world.

He serves on the Bishop's Council for the Full Gospel Baptist Church Fellowship and is the Bishop of Evangelism. He is married to Dr. Diane G. Walker, DDS.